SKILLED TRADE CAREER PLANNING FOR TEENS

THE HANDBOOK OF LUCRATIVE SKILLED TRADES &
HIGH PAYING OCCUPATIONS THAT DON'T REQUIRE
EXPENSIVE COLLEGE DEGREES

P.D. MASON

SUGARDOG PUBLISHING

To the generations of hardworking, skilled tradespeople who have endlessly kept our world running smoothly, we are eternally grateful for your dedication.

In a very general way, our society has fallen out of love with the skilled trades. Part of the problem is a myriad of myths and misperceptions that surround the jobs themselves, but the biggest cause is our stubborn belief that a four-year degree is the best path for most people.

— MIKE ROWE

CONTENTS

INTRODUCTION

Hello again, readers! Thank you for choosing Skilled Trade Career Planning For Teens as your next book to read. This is the third and final book in my Career Planning For Teens collection, and if you have read *Financially Smart Career Planning For Teens* (SugarDog Publishing, 2023) or *Apprenticeship Career Planning For Teens* (SugarDog Publishing, 2023), I humbly thank you for supporting me again by reading this final book.

If you haven't read either of the two prequels to this book, you won't need to go back and read those first. Although the three books were written in somewhat of a sequential order, starting with the first book isn't essential.

The collection of the three books is intended to be "the big picture" of the information you likely haven't received in your high school career planning curriculum, so although I would suggest you read each of the three books in the series, the order in which you read them is not really that important. However, the big picture isn't fully understood without reading all three books, as each has its part to play in the Career Planning For Teens topic.

The books are designed for you to make an educated decision when deciding whether a college path is right for you or whether you'd like to explore a viable option that hundreds of young men and women before you have researched and found great success.

This book is intended to familiarize you with the "skilled trades" in the United States. Skilled trades, in a nutshell, means you have been trained in and are working in a career that provides a specific "hands-on skill" to the workforce, such as plumbing, nursing assistant, software code writing, welding, cyber security, auto mechanic, etc.

Hundreds (if not more) of skilled trades are available, and most trades (I use trades and skilled trades interchangeably quite often, just FYI) have very affordable schooling options. By very affordable, I mean at a fraction of the cost of a four-year college path.

Some experts and financial reporting websites have estimated that a vocational career education can provide savings of upwards of 70-80 thousand dollars over a typical four years of college, and that is something you absolutely should consider as you're approaching your last years of high school and have some career planning decisions ahead of you.

Please keep an open mind when reading this book that the skilled trades have existed in some form or another for centuries. If the trades weren't lucrative and weren't a worthwhile avenue to make a great living with great benefits, there wouldn't have been hundreds of thousands of people who retired financially secure from those trades over the last hundreds of years.

If you haven't read the first two books in the series, you aren't aware that I've shared bits and pieces of my background and how I ended up in the skilled trades. I've shared just a bit in each of the first books, and now in this book, I'll go into a bit more detail on my career, the successes I've had, and, in retrospect, how my path in the skilled trades was unique and ultimately came with some hardships for my family - but well worth it.

As I tell you a bit more about how I developed my career in the trades, I'll paraphrase some of the previous things I've written in the first two books.

I grew up in the suburbs of a major metropolitan city in the Midwest. My dad was blue-collar, and he was a hardworking plumber. My mother was a homemaker and stayed at home to raise my siblings and me. I would never say our family was wealthy, but we lived in a nice suburban neighborhood, and being a 1980s teenager in the suburbs was great.

We were the typical blue-collar family. My dad worked hard, kept an immaculate lawn, and took care of all the upgrades to the house on weekends. My mom ran the household and prepared a family dinner every night. Pretty typical for a working-class family.

After my older siblings went to college, my folks' relationship broke down. My younger sibling and I had an age difference of six years, so during that time, my folks' primary focus was making sure the younger sibling was cared for, leaving me to fend for myself in many situations.

Fast forward to my mid-teens, I entered my junior year of high school and initially did very well. At nearly eighteen years old, I became pretty lost and started falling behind in school, but I nonetheless made it through that year.

Just before my senior year of high school started that fall, I decided to drop out of high school as I was finally eighteen and would move out of state. A few weeks before quitting high school, I remember telling my dad that I planned to quit high school and move on, and his only comment was, "Well, your mother is going to be disappointed." I don't fault my dad for that lackadaisical attitude; it wasn't until many years later that I realized it was unknowingly a pivotal moment for me. Had my dad tried to talk me out of that decision, my life plausibly could have landed in an entirely different orbit than where I am now.

In retrospect of that decision to quit high school, I really never considered the implications of dropping out of high school at eighteen years old and setting out on my own with no resources. I didn't even have my own car at that point and moved out of state without any job prospects in the state I was headed for.

I talk about decision-making as a young adult quite a bit in my second book in this series, *Apprenticeship Carrer Planning For Teens.* Although many years after I dropped out of high school, I would preach to my own children about the importance of graduating from high school, those retrospective bad decision "dots" I created as an eighteen-year-old young man stick with me today as the right choice at the time. I'll tell you in detail about the "dots" I'm referencing later in this book.

I struggled for the next five or six years after quitting high school. Although somewhere in that time period, I had completed my GED, I wasn't educated in anything other than trying to find a job that paid more than the job I was currently in. I didn't have a plan for my life that day I quit high school, and it would catch up to me a few years later.

A half dozen or so years after I told my dad I was dropping out of high school, he sat me down for a stern conversation about my life's direction (or lack of direction). My dad told me I needed to join the same apprenticeship an Uncle of his had told him to join, as years before that conversation, my dad had gotten married and started a family with very few career prospects. My dad had told me to take the time in the apprenticeship to learn the job skills and become educated in the apprenticeship school.

He also told me that if I didn't like the job when I graduated from that apprenticeship, I would at least have a steady income while trying to figure out what I wanted to do. I listened to my dad and joined a plumbing apprenticeship, and although I wasn't quite sure at the time that becoming a plumber was something I wanted to do for the rest of my life, I never looked back.

My career in plumbing might be a bit of a non-traditional career path for most plumbers. I spent the beginning of my career honing my skills in an apprenticeship and continued learning on the job after that. After about a dozen or so years in the field, I had the itch to do more. Did I like what I was doing day in and day out? *Sure, you could say I liked it.* Every day, I wanted to stand back at the end of the day and see what I had crafted or built from a pile of pipe and fittings.

Did I appreciate getting really dirty sometimes? *Maybe not so much, but it was a condition of the job.* Sometimes, a Plumber gets into messy situations, and they get dirty. It wasn't ever a big deal for me. Plumbing came easily to me, and sometimes, it was almost mindless. That's likely where the itch to do more came in.

After those dozen years in the field, I found a project management & estimating job for a local contractor. I hadn't ever thought about becoming a project manager in the plumbing field, just as I hadn't ever considered pursuing that side of the construction business. I didn't know much anything about project management, so at that time, I was venturing out of the comfort zone of my regular day-to-day duties as a licensed plumber. The talks I give these days to new apprentices about the different directions their careers can take them usually include a topic of project management, and I tell the new apprentices that as they progress through their careers, they're going to become very proficient at figuring out job costs in their head - therefore the estimating side of project management should be a breeze.

I tell the apprentices that just like clockwork, it's going to happen that a relative might call them (scratch that - will call them) when a water heater needs to be replaced, or Great Aunt Esther bought a new faucet from the big box home store. Great Aunt Esther would like you to come over and install the faucet, and she will pay you for your time. That's basically the estimating side of Project Management - estimating the costs and what your time is worth to help Great

Aunt Esther and then figuring out how much profit you'd like over and above the costs to put in her faucet.

Plumbers are always asked, "How much to do this?" or "What would you charge me to do that?". That's how I knew that even though I was well outside of my comfort zone, I was interested in moving toward project management in my career. I didn't need a Bachelor's degree of something to move into the business side of plumbing; I just had to know my job and rely on my education and my knowledge of the industry to be successful.

I've spent the past fifteen years or so of my career in a project management role, estimating projects large and small and running those projects from start to finish. I've had projects that made bundles of money for the employer I was working for, and I've also had a few losers. The losers, thankfully, were very minimally considered losers. As I explain to new apprentices about project management, if a job makes a dollar, the job makes money, right? And that's really the only job requirement of a project manager - to generate revenue for the employer.

I've worn other hats in the industry, like Supervisor and Field Superintendent (also called a General Foreman), and I've been fortunate throughout my career to have had an apprenticeship education and excellent hands-on trainers when I was in my on-the-job training years. I also ran my own plumbing business for several years when the housing market crashed and the US economy took a downturn leading up to the recession in the late 2000s.

My apprenticeship education focused on commercial installation, service, and repair in plumbing. Undoubtedly, the job training and education I received allowed me to push myself into different aspects of my occupation that I didn't know I had a knack for.

My 26-year career has brought me all over the United States for work and has allowed me to become a Master Plumber in multiple states. I wouldn't have had the opportunity to wear all of these hats in a skilled trade career had I not pushed myself many times out of my comfort zone of just going to work every day and then going home. I was driven to succeed, and bringing value to each employer I worked for was my main goal - as that was what I figured would set me apart from the crowd. Looking back on my career, that first decision to leave my comfort zone and take on unfamiliar tasks and elements of the industry set me apart from the crowd. That's when I really learned the meaning of "value" in relation to what you can bring to the table in your career.

I realized several years ago that I had an interest in molding and shaping the next generation of skilled trade workers (not necessarily plumbers), and that is how I became an instructor at the local apprenticeship school, where I teach apprentices a few evenings a week during the school year.

I have advocated for high-school students like yourself for many years, and my advocacy has centered around educating them about non-traditional career paths. Unfortunately, I read statistics every day about how many high school-age students go off to college and, somewhere along the way, realize college wasn't all it's cracked up to be, and then those former college students get saddled with tens of thousands of dollars in student loan debt.

If those students could have been informed about the complete picture of available career options after high school, the for-profit college system would have an entirely different landscape.

Without a doubt, I can assure you that occupations in skilled trades provide an excellent career alternative without having to agonize over choosing a college and incur the student loan debt that oftentimes comes with a college experience. Skilled trade educations enable you to be career-ready, the jobs pay very well, and skilled trades jobs often have benefits packages and retirement programs that many non-trade workers wish for.

If you've read either of my two previous books on this Career Planning For Teens topic, you already know that I'm a career-skilled tradesperson who has worked in the construction industry for more than a quarter-century. In my two previous books, I've given you minor details of my apprenticeship and my career here and there, and I assure you by the time you reach the end of this book, you'll have the complete picture of how this high school dropout and two-time college dropout found success. First through an earn while you learn apprenticeship, and next, through a quarter century of pushing myself beyond what I thought my capabilities were in a skilled trade career.

We will cover a lot of information in this book, providing the remainder of the "full picture" I set out to give you when I wrote Financially Smart Career Planning For Teens (SugarDog Publishing, 2023). When writing that book, many additional talking points came up where I felt it necessary to include more information than there was space available in the book, and that's where the other book ideas were born.

Skilled Trade Career Planning for Teens will introduce you to the skilled trades in a very comprehensive way. This introduction to the trades will guide you through the many skilled trades available and the industries those skilled trades are in.

You'll become familiar with the typical duties of a skilled tradesperson, and you'll also come to understand why the skilled trades are a great career path and an alternative option to a four-year college degree. You'll learn why women in the skilled trades are just as important as men. Additionally, you understand how everyone in the skilled trades has an equal opportunity to advance their careers - and take their career as far as they want.

I'll debunk almost every myth regarding the trades on topics such as yearly earnings, the typical skilled tradespersons' education path when entering the occupation, and why people incorrectly think that if someone works in the skilled trades, it means they couldn't get into the college of their choice.

You'll understand that there are numerous educational paths to a skilled trades career, and none of those paths come even close to the cost of a four-year degree from a college.

You will read in detail about the imbalance in the labor workforce as more skilled trade workers retire than replacement skilled workers can be found to replace those retirees, and how beneficial that imbalance is for you as a high school student considering a career in the skilled trades.

There are many more topics we will visit in this book, and I don't want to overload you with information before you even open chapter one, so I'll wrap up the intro to this book by saying; please remember I'm giving you the information in this book from the perspective of a person that has gone before you and discovered all the great things that the trades has to offer.

I'm just a regular guy with a life and a family like you. My day job has always been my focus day in and day out for the last 26 years, as that's the income I need to pay the bills, fix the house, and occasionally take a vacation.

Skilled trades information was not presented in any of the guidance counseling offices I was in during my high school days, and that's why I've written these three books - so you can be informed and make an educated decision on where you want your career to go and how are you going to get there.

Although I did partake in "shop" classes when I was in high school, somewhere around the years 1995 to the early 2000s, high schools across America had a shift in mindset about the importance of vocational options being allowed in high schools. During those years, high schools felt it was a better use of taxpayer money to shed the hands-on courses like auto mechanics or wood shop, and many of those schools also diminished their music programs.

At the time, the high school administration mindset was that students needed fewer elective courses (like a shop class or music class) and more general education classes to prepare their student bodies better to enter college - which was their mistake. The mindset that high schools were in would change the career guidance landscape for years in high schools across America.

Although I have heard of a few high schools once again creating hands-on shop classes, it is only a reactive measure to the general public's dismay that for so many years, the high school career planning curriculums only revolved around college and nothing else.

We are approaching the mid-2020s, and it is a great time to consider a skilled trade as a career path instead of a career that requires a four-year college degree simply because of skyrocketing college costs that are crippling to young adults like yourself.

With that, my friends, I'll let you turn the page and start chapter one.

WELCOME TO THE SKILLED TRADES

WHAT ARE SKILLED TRADES?

When I searched for a definition of "skilled trade," nothing was found using that combination of words. However, the Merriam-Webster dictionary definition of *Skilled* is: 1) having acquired mastery of or skill in something (such as a technique or a trade), and 2) of, relating to, or requiring workers or labor with skill and training in a particular occupation, craft, or trade.

I will take a stab at a real-world definition of "skilled trades," but I'll need to skilled-trade-speak it for you in hopes you have a complete understanding as we start this first chapter. "Skilled Trade" means that you have been trained in a specific occupation, and different occupations perform different tasks. Your training is acquired most often through an apprenticeship school or vocational school. You further your education and skills building while working in that occupation with an experienced worker or trainer who will provide oversight and guidance as you progress through your learning period, and then you will start your autonomous career working in the skilled trades.

Another easy way to explain the skilled trades is simply: occupations that require experience-based knowledge, training, and skills. Skilled trades jobs are almost always hands-on type jobs, and although most trades workers have occupations in the construction industry, there are also many beneficial careers in industries outside of construction.

Multiple different terms mean or have a meaning similar to "skilled trades," and for the remainder of this book, I will refer to the trades, skilled trades, technical trades, or any other trade-specific type occupation as "the trades" or "skilled trades." I will talk a lot, and I mean a lot, about education in this book, as you can't survive in a technical or skilled field of work without being educated in that field. I dive much deeper into education opportunities in the trades in later chapters.

As we continue throughout this book, when I'm referencing schooling or education, I typically will reference anything having to do with education as "trade school" generally, unless the topic is specific to vocational school, technical college, or technical school (which are three different ways of referencing a technical educational institution). In the case of those three, I will specify which schooling I'm referencing.

You might already be asking, "Well, where does the 'trade' part of skilled trades come in then"? I don't have a simple answer for that other than when the words "skilled" and "trades" are used as a term; the consensus is someone is talking about an occupation requiring a particular skill, ability, or knowledge that may be obtained through college, vocational or technical school, or specialized training such as an apprenticeship with the corresponding apprenticeship schooling.

If you were to take a look at any technical or vocational school certificate or diploma program list, the majority of the program offerings could be considered skilled trade, as you are gaining the technical knowledge and training, skillset, and technical hands-on aptitude to perform a specific set of job duties out in the workforce.

By today's standards, many classifiable trades exist in the US, UK, and Canada. These trades are from various industries and sectors, and more occupations are likely considered a trade than you'd initially consider.

Skilled trades jobs are in extremely high demand at the time of the publication of this book, as the outlook for job security and job growth for hands-on blue-collar type occupations is on a considerable incline due to so many in the baby-boomer generation approaching retirement age. The exit of the older generation from the trades jobs leaves an even more significant gap in the workforce as for the past three decades; there also has been an "open call" of sorts for recruits into trades jobs - as even the past three decades has seen slow growth. The retirements, coupled with the slow (but gaining) interest in the skilled trades, provide for an almost sure bet that anyone seeking to work in a field considered a trade should have no problem securing a well-paying, lifelong career.

A study by The Harris Poll on behalf of Express Employment Professionals is an additional marker for the thought process that trades jobs will continue to fall short of full employment for the next half-century. The study reported that in 2019 the United States birth rate hit a 32-year low. This means that in 2037, the United States will see the lowest turnout of post-high school workforce-ready young adults in recent history. Based on this statistic, the disproportionate retirement rate compared to new skilled workers entering the trades will continue to suffer a shortfall for decades.

I can't stress it enough: skilled trades occupations are available, skilled trades employers are begging for a replacement workforce, and a skilled trade career choice will provide a lifetime of work and excellent pay.

GREAT CAREER PATH

If you've read my previous book "Apprenticeship Career Planning For Teens," you already know that it was my Father who sat me down one day and made no apologies for telling me he was tired of seeing me seemingly floating without a landing zone and "gently" suggested I apply for the same apprenticeship he went through. I followed his gentle nudge, and a few decades later, I woke up one day and realized how different my life could have been had my dad not given me that nudge. I guess it's safe to say I owe the start of my career to my dad, and what I did with my career, I owe all to myself. I will tell you more about that in later in this book.

Aside from the reasons I've already mentioned about why the trades are a good career choice, like great pay and benefits, there are some often not-thought-about reasons why a career in the trades is nearly a no-brainer.

High demand for workers. We've touched on this already, and I think I clarified just how much of a deficit there is in the skilled trades workforce. There are regular projections made by the US Government and private companies alike, and data shows that the need for professional, skilled, and technically trained workers has not met the requests for those workers in decades.

Minimal education cost. Vocational schools, technical schools, and apprenticeship training programs all provide the required training for a successful career in the skilled trades. The US Government may provide government-sponsored grants to new workers or people looking to make a career shift to attend vocational school to gain the class-room hours required for some skilled trade occupations. It's not uncommon for young adults looking to enter the skilled trade workforce to receive their training without ever paying a dime for such training.

Advancement Potential. Depending on the occupation within a skilled trade and the industry in which that trade serves, there's often an opportunity for rapid career advancement. People have the misconception that if you work a skilled trade job, you are doing the same thing every day, day after day. I can tell you with certainty that is not the case. Imagine being an Electrician, and your only job for the next thirty or so years after you entered the trade was to put faceplates on electrical outlets. Aside from likely being recognized as the best faceplate installer in your commu-nity, would you think it was a worthwhile career? I think not, and that would be a dull existence for a person. Don't get me wrong, I know there are hard-working people in industries such as manufacturing that stand at a machine, push a few buttons, and watch a brand new widget pop out of that machine, and that's what they do day in and day out. Some people enjoy that type of work (or the stability from that work, knowing that the widget market will never falter), so they'll likely have a job for life. Job stability means job security, which is imperative for most adult working people. In skilled trades jobs, job security is there, and it always has been

Great pay structure. New skilled trades workers are often paid a healthy wage right from the beginning of their careers. Wages differ between skilled trades, and that's to be expected as each trade has a different set of job conditions, knowledge base requirements, or safety or health elements. It's not uncommon for a recent graduate from a vocational school with a certificate in a skilled trade program to enter the workforce with a base starting pay in the neighborhood of 60 or 70 thousand dollars a year. If you entered the trades through an apprenticeship, that's a bit of a different pay structure, which we will discuss later. Skilled trades positions often require additional certifications, or as technology advances, it's not uncommon for a trade worker to get other certificates or credentials as their career moves on.

Those credentials are worth something to an employer, so the employer typically would compensate you accordingly for holding those credentials. Quite often, when a worker has new certifications to offer the employer, it means that the employer can expand their business offering to include the work of that certification, which means the employer will generate more revenue, and a portion of that revenue added to the employers' bottom line typically would get passed along to you as the certification holder. Most skilled trades have a fantastic pay structure, which includes an hourly wage and "fringe" benefits. Fringe benefits are extra benefits supplementing an employee's salary or wage. Examples of fringe benefits include health care, pension or 401K contributions, meal plans, travel pay, etc.

Avoidance of student loan debt. As most trades jobs are technical, the need for a four-year college degree is almost non-existent. As an 18-year-old soon-to-be high school graduate, you could enter the skilled trades directly out of high school. There is no need to enter the traditional college system and take general education courses for a skilled trade, which means you'll never have to endure years of student loan payments, which take a healthy bite out of your monthly income. As I've said in my previous two career planning books, the financial freedom from deciding to enter the workforce in a skilled trade occupation is nearly immeasurable due to the entry requirements of being eighteen years old and having a high school diploma or GED. As you start your career, avoiding student loan debt will financially propel you years ahead of your peers. I have known many young adults who began their careers right after high school commencement and have gone on to purchase their first house around age 22 or 23, just 4 or 5 years after graduating high school. I've also known young adults of the same age who struggle to find an entry-level job in their college degree field. The opportunities that result from deciding to forego the traditional college path and enter the workforce as a skilled tradesperson are undoubtedly worthwhile.

Prideful work. Many skilled tradespeople I've talked to over the years regularly comment that one of the things they like best about their career choice is the ability to stand back at the end of the day and think to themselves, "Look at that; I built that." Skilled tradespeople are prideful people, and that's where the technical aspect of skilled trades work comes in. Working in a trade means you often create a finished product from a pile of bits and pieces. Those bits and pieces are usually the materials you need to create the finished product, and that's what drives many skilled trade workers, as creativity often goes hand in hand with those occupations. Trades workers have different functions when constructing a building, maintaining an oil refinery, building an ocean fairing ship, fixing an elevator, or even sweeping a floor. You may have heard the term "it takes a village" at some time in your life, and that term means that everyone has a role (or plays a part) in the bigger picture. Skilled tradespeople are the epitome of respectful, helpful, and team players. I regularly see different trades working together to get all or part of a project done, as it benefits multiple trades to collaborate while working towards the larger overall goal.

Working Hours. Depending on the industry you are working in, the work hours are fantastic. As I am in the construction industry, I'll use that industry as an example. Most skilled trade jobs happen during daylight hours; I know that's pretty general, but let's say 6 a.m. to 6 p.m. Buildings typically can't be constructed during nighttime hours, so working during the day makes sense. Construction trades in the US are semi-regional for certain job conditions, and in my area of the Midwest, sunrise during the summer is typically right around 6 a.m. I know many trades workers who prefer their eight-hour work day from 6 a.m. to 2:30 p.m. I also know many who might have children who go to daycare, so those people like to start their eight-hour day at 7 a.m. I've found that most skilled trade contracting companies are very accommodating to working hours as long as the job is getting done. An eight-hour day is typical and has been for my entire career. I appreciate starting my day at 6 a.m. and being home mid-afternoon as I might also have things I want to do at home that day. Of course, this is not a rule or a regulation, but most skilled trade occupations work 8 hours a day Monday through Friday, and unless the job requires some weekend overtime, weekends are usually non-working days. In full transparency, overtime happens now and again, and even on weekends if the job requires it. Most importantly, you'll be notified in advance if overtime is needed; if you work over-time, you get paid overtime.

The seven reasons above barely explain why a skilled trade job is a good career choice. As we continue through the book, I'll explain many more reasons why you cannot go wrong choosing a career in the trades.

If you are a high school student considering entering the skilled trades occupations, there are a few specific things you should be aware of that might also help your decision-making process. As a high school student, you can enter the skilled trades occupations as long as you are at least eighteen years old on the day after your commencement from high school or the day you start working in a trade. Ideally, this would be through an apprenticeship program, but that is not always the only way to gain employment in the trade. Below are five items that make a solid case to consider entering a skilled trade right after high school.

Hands-on experience. As a newly graduated young adult entering the workforce, there is no better time to enter an apprenticeship or an occupation that pays you to learn on the job. Most skilled trades jobs provide all of the on-the-job training you will need to succeed in the workforce, in addition to a low-cost education program that goes hand in hand with your on-the-job training.

Cost benefit. Unlike many post-high school expensive college programs, skilled trades education is very affordable. A skilled trade education path may cost less than USD 1,000 yearly or be as high as $ 2,500 annually, depending on the industry and trade you are working in. An average skilled trade apprenticeship program education costs USD 5,000 or less overall during the duration of the apprenticeship. The skilled trades training and education programs are quite different than a traditional for-profit college program in that the majority of the cost for your skilled trade education may be for incidentals, like books, or it may be for technology items like a laptop or a tablet. An alternate option to the multi-year apprenticeship is to enroll in a vocational or technical college program to fast track your skilled trade education. In that case, that program may cost upwards of USD 10,000, as getting your education through a technical school means you are somewhat jumpstarting your career by completing your education first. That choice, which is a good choice, comes with a bit of a cost over an apprenticeship, which is a longer-term from start to finish to get your education.

Additionally, another benefit to a few years of vocational school before entering the workforce is you'd likely come out of vocational school with whichever credentials you needed to work in your selected occupation, which means you've cut a considerable amount of time off of the typical on-the-job training program. For example, there are two ways to become an HVAC technician in my area. The first way is a person can sign up with one of the local apprenticeship programs and work in an earn while learning apprenticeship under the direction of a credentialed HVAC journey worker who will train you to do everything there is to do as a technician. After a certain number of years in an apprenticeship, that person will become a credentialed HVAC technician and be at full journeyworker pay.

The second way is that a person could enroll in a two-year program at a local vocational school in an HVAC service program. Throughout that two-year program, that person will gain all the relevant knowledge needed to perform that HVAC technician job. What the person doesn't have, however, is the hours spent on the job applying what they learned in school to real-world scenarios. This is not a bad thing; it is, however, potentially a drawback to the vocational school route as a person working in the trades needs to have classroom and on-the-job experience to apply the knowledge learned to the hands-on tasks. The choice is yours, which route to a skilled trade career you'd pursue, and each route has plusses and minuses that come with them.

The demand for skilled workers is real. I've already told you multiple times how upsidedown the workforce is for the skilled trades, so I probably don't need to say to you again. However, to drive the point home - I'll let you know that it will be many decades, possibly ten decades (that's 100 years) before enough interested people enter a skilled trade occupation to reverse the effects of the current imbalance in the labor outlook. For years, the "blue collar" work carried a stigma as people thought trades workers were uneducated or unmotivated. I can tell you with certainty those conversations years ago are what the industries have been battling for years. The battle has been to de-stigmatize trade work, and although it is happening, it's very slow to gain some traction. Skilled trade workers are anything but uneducated. For what it's worth, the typical skilled trade worker puts as many hours into their classroom training as a four-year bachelor's degree requires. There are national and state-level requirements regarding how many hours of in-classroom training tradespeople must attend. Although I don't know the numbers for every trade, I can assure you it approaches 2,000 classroom hours overall while in an apprenticeship for a skilled trade. Think about that: a skilled tradesperson has to sit in class for as many hours as a Harvard graduate in a four-year program but at a fraction of the cost that a Harvard grad paid for an education. The demand for workers is there; it's real, and as long as there's a demand, the price of the education you need to perform that skilled trade occupation will remain very affordable and likely without the need to take debilitating student loans.

Technological literacy. The skilled trades are moving into an era entirely new to how it's been done for years. The technological advancements I've seen in the last quarter century have blown my mind, yet some tradespeople consider technological progress a threat to their work and livelihood. In contrast, I view it as the advancement of the world to perform job functions efficiently and cost-effectively. Here's a quick example: I'd consider myself an "old school" type of skilled tradesperson who also loves technology. As a skilled tradesman, I've seen technology enhance industries beyond expectations. When I started my career, if I were sent to a job site to start working, it was typical that someone would hand me a rolled-up set of blueprints for that project that might take me a few days to read through and familiarize myself with. In 2023, paper blueprints are no longer the preferred method for communicating construction documents to field workers. We are heavily into a digital age in 2023, and the construction industry is following suit in a manner that a field technician on a construction job site will only need one item to construct that project to the required specifications - and that one item is a device with internet access. Much of the construction industry has been streamlined to function "in the cloud," and most of the construction industry today is following suit. There's a plethora of online construction coordination applications accessed from a laptop or a tablet, meaning every single person working on that project has immediate access to changes on blueprints, specifications, and even project questions raised by an individual trade. Technological advancement in the skilled trades workforce is here and isn't going away. Studies have been done for years on how technological advancement affects a workforce, and experts are saying that the most recent two generations of workforce-ready adults are poised to be the most qualified to embrace the technology and propel that tech beyond expectations. Top Employers Institute, A Netherlands company that fosters relationships between large employers and their employees states that as of 2023, Millennials (born 1981-1996) are "Tech Savvy" and Gen Z's (born 1997-2012) are "Tech Native". Although Millennials have been in the workforce for about 15 years, they indeed had a hand in advancing the technology used in the trades today. Their contribution to the discussion regarding technology in the trades was certainly met without resistance.

The millennial generation quickly picked up on that tech and effectively incorporated it into their daily work lives without skipping a beat. Gen Z, however, is a different story. The Gen Z generation was born into technology. They may have had smartphones in their hand in elementary school. When mom or dad needed just a few minutes of downtime, the babysitter named iPad might have taken over. Gen Z is the technological generation, and they likely were surrounded by tech every year of their childhood and young adult school years. Suppose you are a Generation Z young adult thinking about your future. In that case, you should consider the trades, as there's a perfect chance you will propel yourself into a career that seamlessly integrates with your "born with" knowledge of technology and how that tech plays a part in the everyday lives of working adults.

Job satisfaction. The website ANGI (formerly Angie's List in the US) reports that the "great resignation" of the COVID-19 pandemic affected almost every industry and every sector of business - except the skilled trades. The great resignation evolved as many countries were closing their borders, working from home, and just trying to stay afloat financially without the regular business practices they were used to. People weren't happy at their jobs, whether working from home or not. People felt their work-life balance was way off, and their employers weren't attempting to rectify those feelings. Wikipedia reports even more reasons why the adult workforce was making snap decisions to leave their jobs, which included a lack of benefits packages and an unequal pay structure to the rising cost of living. Throughout many reports on the great resignation (also called the "Big Quit" and the "Great Reshuffle"), there was one thing that remained constant within those reports - that 83% of skilled trade workers remained happy and satisfied working in a trade while many others in the country were jumping ship for proverbial greener pastures. Additionally, only 0.05% of tradespeople feel unsatisfied with their current skilled traces career. A career in the skilled trades brings a lifetime of work that provides many opportunities for creativity, networking, and advancement.

THE MYTHS AND STIGMA ABOUT SKILLED TRADES

Big Business

Stanley Black & Decker, the tool company responsible for producing brands such as DeWalt, Black+Decker, Craftsman, Stanley, Cub Cadet, Troy-Bilt, and more, has felt the effects of the skilled labor shortage for years. The company released a report that stated possibilities of why the skilled labor shortage can't seem to pick up enough steam to close the gap on that shortage.

The report states that many high school students commented that skilled trades are a great career choice, but only 16% of those students stated they would consider a skilled trades occupation. The report further says that nearly 60% of those surveyed had never thought about talking to someone about skilled trades as an alternative to college. The main objective points in the report go on to say that even though in just one sector alone - construction, as of mid-2022, there were over 650,000 unfilled jobs available, with seemingly no interested people to fill those positions.

Stanley Black & Decker concludes the report by summarizing that the skilled labor shortage will remain constant until a few key points of thought are addressed and discussed, which might provide open communication about how lucrative and sustainable the skilled trade sectors are and not specifically revolve around construction.

Stanley Black & Decker is a power and lawn tool manufacturing company valued at nearly USD 16 Billion. When a $16B company is venturing into the conversation of skilled trades, and the lack of understanding by high school students of how important it is to consider these as viable career choices, it surely means that even a behemoth of a manufacturing company has "skin-in-the-game" of sorts to make attempts to lure graduating high school students into blue-collar work that doesn't require anything more than a high school diploma or a GED to be successful.

A few of the crossover points Stanley Black & Decker were attempting to get across to people like yourself who may be giving slight consideration to a career in the skilled trades but seem not to have the whole picture are:

There's a general misunderstanding of long-term financial security. When asked in the survey, 81% of young individuals and 78% of parents are worried about the potential expenses of post-high school education. Additionally, 87% of young adults and 93% of parents find the idea of starting a career earlier than completing a four-year degree highly appealing. Exploring the skilled trades can pave the way for young individuals, yet many underestimate the starting earning potential in these fields. Only 42% believe skilled trade workers can make at least $50,000, and a concerning 19% think the starting pay is less than $20,000.

However, half of current skilled trade workers with under ten years of experience earned at least $50,000 yearly when they began their careers. In a recent survey of young individuals, 43% showed much more enthusiasm for pursuing a skilled trade career upon learning a compelling fact: after five years, those who attend trade school and start working can find themselves $140,000 ahead, on average, compared to students enrolling in a traditional four-year college before entering the workforce. This highlights the incredible financial advantage of opting for skilled trades as a career path. So, if you've been uncertain about considering skilled trades, it's time to rethink and consider the lucrative opportunities the trades offer. Start early, earn well, and secure a prosperous future by working in a skilled trade.

There is a lack of knowledge about the required skills. People have long believed that young people don't like skilled trade jobs because they involve physical work. But the facts show that only 12% of the 40% who don't consider skilled trades as a career say it's because they don't want to do physical labor.

They don't consider these careers mainly because they think they don't have the skills or aren't a good fit for the job. To change this, we need to help them understand what skills are really needed for a successful skilled trade career and challenge these wrong ideas.

Also, many young people have old-fashioned ideas about these jobs. Surprisingly, 23% don't think skilled trades use modern technology, and 18% believe these jobs aren't in demand. But that's not true at all. Most workers (89%) use advanced technology, and almost everyone (94%) says these jobs are in high demand.

By correcting these misconceptions and showing how stable and well-paying skilled trade jobs can be, we can encourage a new generation to choose these careers and build a thriving workforce.

Promoting the skilled trades. When young people plan for life after high school, they often turn to familiar sources for advice. These sources include parents (48%), friends and classmates (44%), and teachers (43%). However, regarding jobs in skilled trades, only 42% of students have talked to people who work in these fields. Even more concerning, 37% have never discussed skilled trade careers with anyone. This lack of communication is why only 29% of young people feel well-informed about how to start a career in skilled trades.

Media and entertainment have a big impact on the careers people choose. More than 60% of workers in skilled trades with less than ten years of experience say that various types of media (like newspapers, websites, social media, and ads) played a big role in helping them decide on their careers. The internet (32%) and social media (21%) were particularly important in shaping their career choices.

To bridge the gap between young people and skilled trade careers, we must connect them with professionals in these fields. By encouraging more conversations and connections with skilled trade workers, we can help the next generation make informed decisions about their careers. Also, showing positive and accurate portrayals of skilled trades in the media can inspire young people to explore the opportunities in these growing industries.

Skilled trades are male-dominated. There are clear differences in how young men and young women think about skilled trade careers. Surveys show that more young men (53%) know about these careers than young women (36%). Also, when young men think about their future jobs, more of them (64%) consider skilled trades, while fewer young women (49%) do. Young men (69%) also find skilled trade careers more appealing than young women (52%).

These differences in thinking also extend to parents. Men and women have similar opinions about whether skilled trade careers offer good job options, but men are more than twice as likely as women to consider these careers for their kids.

To address the shortage of skilled workers, involving and empowering women is important. They need to know about the opportunities and benefits of skilled trade careers. By promoting equal opportunities and removing gender barriers, we can create a diverse and inclusive workforce, which will help solve the shortage of skilled workers.

The idea that women don't belong in skilled trades is rapidly fading. Skilled trades aren't just for men or women; if you can do the job, you'll do well in the long run.

MYTHS

For years, there has been a stigma that a person who works in the skilled trades wasn't very smart in school. Or, that person was viewed as unmotivated to succeed and just took any job that came along.

These types of stigmatizing thoughts aren't anything new, and these thoughts (whether had by young adults or working adults) will continue to be attached to blue-collar skilled trades work for decades, I'm sure of that.

If you've read either of my two previous books on this topic, you will have already read some of my de-stigmatizing of the trades. If you're new to the series, I will cover some stigmatizing myths that are nothing more than the perception of people who don't fully understand the opportunities a skilled trade offers.

Myth #1 - *A skilled trades job doesn't pay well, and high-paying jobs require a four-year degree.* **This is FALSE.** Many skilled trade occupations pay more per working hour than careers that require a four-year degree. Additionally, most four-year degree holders will likely carry a student loan debt that starts on average six months after college commencement.

Most skilled trade occupations start from an apprenticeship, which inherently means the cost of schooling is at a minimum compared to a four-year college path.

Myth #2 - *Skilled trade jobs are strenuous and dirty.* **This is FALSE.** This stigmatizing theory that skilled trade work is harsh and dirty, mindless hard labor, and incredibly dull "assembly line" like environments is inaccurate and highly outdated. Skilled trades require hands-on work that sometimes can be considered physical labor, which is why many tradespeople enjoy the work. With regular advancements in technology to streamline the performance and safety of manual labor jobs, the severely strenuous work is all but gone. Here's an example: You already know that I've been a plumber by trade for the last quarter century. My father was a plumber before me, and one of my children also followed in our footsteps and decided to become a plumber. Before my father retired, he would install heavy cast iron pipes that no person should be carrying or hoisting into ceilings by themselves, yet he did it as "that's what we did back then" (his words). Fast forward a few decades when heavy cast iron plumbing pipes were replaced by lighter and easier-to-manage PVC pipes that served the same purpose as the heavy cast iron piping. New material, better efficiency. I rarely see the heavy cast iron piping being installed anymore as it just doesn't make sense from an efficiency standpoint for one, and for two, it's very strenuous to install that pipe.

Here's example number two: For years after the new lighter and easier PVC pipe came to the market, plumbers would virtually line up to dig the trenches in the ground that these pipes would lay in as they could dig a trench and connect the PVC pipes in such a speedy manner that they were considered hard and fast workers as a lot of pipes could get installed in a short amount of time. I told you my child was a plumber, and in a recent conversation with my child, I learned that a new way of installing that PVC pipe in the ground is using a machine called a "trencher."

A trenching machine is a walk-behind machine resembling a chainsaw on wheels, although the saw mechanism is much larger than a traditional chainsaw and has large toothed outcroppings that dig the dirt up and out of the trench. According to my child, these machines have variable depth settings and are one of the innovative ways companies are attempting to become more efficient.

These examples are about how the skilled trades evolve, and always for the better. There's not one person cracking a whip at the workers to work harder and faster, and no one is going home at the end of the day feeling ready to heave over and not make it to work the next day. Yes, skilled trades take a bit of muscle and ingenuity here and there, but you are paid very well for your labor and ideas.

Myth #3 - *Skilled trades occupations are for people who didn't get good grades in high school.* **Again, This is FALSE.** While working in most skilled trades, a person has to have a solid foundation in math, reading, and writing. Some science helps, but not always required. Working in the skilled trades means you'll do the math, like calculating the square feet in a room to purchase and install the right amount of carpet. You'll also likely be writing emails or text messages to a supervisor to communicate needs on a job. You'll also probably look at paper or digital schematics or blueprints, where good reading skills are handy as many blueprint notes need to be understood.

Myth #4 - *There's no career advancement in the trades.* **Once again** - **FALSE.** In the introduction of this book, I shared that I've had a successful career in skilled trades. Not every job I had was a chance for career growth, but because I was determined to succeed, my career took me to positions I never imagined when I started out as a young tradesman.

I always wondered, "What can I do to add more value to my employer?" These thoughts kept me consistently employed in the skilled trades. In the trades, your career can go as far as you want it to. You just need to set goals that open up new opportunities.

As I write this book, I feel like I've reached the pinnacle of my career, as I've worked in almost every role as a plumber in the field and in many positions on the business side of mechanical contracting companies. Now, in my last decade before retirement, I don't think I can climb any higher on the career ladder than I already have. I'm proud and satisfied with my career, although it wasn't always easy. I learned something from each experience, and the knowledge I gained from each new experience in my career was the value I brought to each employer.

Myth #5 - *It's not consistent income and is very seasonal.* **FALSE.** Although some regions of the US have to endure long, cold winters, most skilled trades (specifically construction trades) do not come to a grinding halt. As skilled trades in severely hot climates are acclimated and prepared to work in extreme weather conditions, so is most of the country prepared to work in their respective climates. Nearly all trades work throughout the year as those trades adjust for job conditions, such as weather.

Myth #6 - *Working a skilled trades job is dangerous.* Again, **FALSE.** In the quarter century since I started working in the trades, I have seen much advancement by OSHA (Occupational Safety and Health Administration) in the US. OSHA regularly visits all industries served by skilled trades to ensure workplace safety is being upheld. There's a lot of misinformation regarding what the purpose of OSHA is. In my career, I've seen many safety updates to everyday tasks performed and have seen multiple industries push for stronger OSHA training within the trades. When I first started as an apprentice, it wasn't required for apprentices to have any OSHA safety training.

Throughout the years, I've seen the requirements for OSHA training in apprenticeships start as OSHA 10 (meaning that the apprentice has had at least ten hours of career safety training), which led to OSHA 15. OSHA 30, and currently, in 2023, there is an option for an apprentice or a skilled trade worker to become OSHA 60 certified. The OSHA 60 is not a general requirement in most trades; however, I have known tradespeople take it upon themselves to take the OSHA 60 courses on their own accord and then land a skilled trade position as a safety supervisor overseeing a company safety program. Do you know what that's called? Career Advancement.

Myth #7 - *Women can't hack a skilled trades career.* This is one of the biggest **FALSEHOODS** of all. I have worked alongside many women in the trades, and I've seen some of the best hands-on work come from women. I will tell you with authority that women work just as hard as men, often harder, as they naturally feel they need to prove themselves. I also know many men who have changed their mindset over the years about working shoulder to shoulder with women, as those men have also seen what I've seen, and women can do the same math, read a tape measure the same, and pull the trigger on a power tool the same as a male tradesperson does. Although it has taken some time for the mindset to shift regarding women in the trades, many organizations are now celebrating the number of women joining the skilled trades.

Myth #8 - *Skilled trade work isn't essential.* Blatantly **FALSE**. The next time you hop in your car and head to the local coffee shop to pick up your grande white macchiato with rice milk and extra foam but gently chilled, whipped, and stirred, count how many buildings you pass as you arrive at the coffee shop drive-through. How many houses? How many apartment buildings? How many hospitals? Were there strip malls, shopping malls, or airports along the way? What about the Motel 6 that leaves the light on for you, any of those? Was there a church or synagogue? Post office? Fast food joint? Every one of these buildings was built using skilled trade labor.

What happens when these buildings reach their "end of useable life" status? They either a) tear them down, and a new building goes in its place, or b) the building gets refurbished and goes back into operation. What type of labor do they use for options A and B? That's right...*skilled trade labor.*

The skilled trades are as crucial as any other career out there, but what the skilled trades have that other jobs don't have is *sustainability*. There is a constant need for new or updated infrastructure in the US, and skilled trades are the only careers that can take on that task.

I hope this first chapter hasn't completely scared you off the notion that skilled trades occupations are not worthy of your consideration. Understandably, there has been a lot of information presented to you already. Hopefully, you've understood that the generations of skilled trades workers before you made healthy careers using their knowledge and skills, and you absolutely can as well.

There's just one more thing I need to add to this first chapter, and it's barely noticeable other than it might factor into your decision of which industry and trade you may seek additional information for.

Until this point in the book, I've referenced the trades as "the trades," or I've called them "skilled trades." As a refresher, I use those terms interchangeably as a trade is inherently by nature "skilled."

Of the many skilled trades, only three typically require state or local municipality-level licensing (not to be confused with certifications). The three skilled trades typically requiring licensure in the US are:

- Electrician
- HVAC Technician/Installer (Includes Pipefitter)
- Plumber

These three trades require licensing by US state or local government agencies because if plumbing, electrical, or HVAC is not installed correctly, it may pose a danger to the health and safety of the general public. These three trades have strict state or municipal codes that must be adhered to, and workers within these three trades have proven their knowledge of the applicable codes by way of passing education and skills-related testing verifying their knowledge.

A governing agency must license workers in these three trades in order for the tradesperson to work autonomously. Typically, these trades start with an apprenticeship. The apprenticeship program for these trades can be as long as five years, and the apprenticeships for these trades train the worker on every aspect of their occupation so each worker can effectively graduate from that apprenticeship and immediately take their licensing test. These skilled trade workers also must adhere to a strict cycle of continuing education classes to keep their trade licenses up to date and ready for renewal. If a trades worker in either of these three trades fails to renew their license or complete their required continuing education, there is a strong possibility they would need to retake the licensing test to continue working in that field.

In most of the United States, HVAC, Electrical, and Plumbing licensing is governed entirely at the state level, whereas just a few states issue licenses based on a municipality or a county level.

As we close out this chapter, I want to reiterate that any trade in any industry you may feel compelled to further research is a wise choice. If I haven't stressed it enough by now, I'll tell you again, a skilled trade career choice is arguably the best decision you could make as a young adult with some career or college choices ahead of you.

In a skilled trade occupation, the in-classroom hours of education needed are nearly equal to those required to receive a four-year degree. The financial savings in getting your career education through an apprenticeship, vocational institution, or directly from a skilled trades employer has been noted as saving a person USD 140,000 over the life of a typical student loan repayment program.

Skilled trades workers typically retire earlier than those in a non-trades career, as skilled trades workers have very healthy and beneficial retirement options provided on their behalf through employer fringe benefit programs. Additionally, many skilled trade workers provide their own supplemental retirement options, such as a Roth Independent Retirement Account (Roth IRA), which will further enhance their retirement income. Skilled trade workers who supplement their employer-sponsored retirement benefits with their own accounts, such as a Roth IRA, can often retire and receive retirement benefits that surpass the yearly pay they received while working in the trades.

As we move into the next chapter, we will discuss many of the most popular skilled trades and the industries those trades serve. I will give a disclaimer; however, there are too many skilled trade occupations available for me to detail every one of them.

As I've alluded to in this chapter you've just read, many people work in the skilled trades, and a high percentage of those work in a tiny percentage of the industries experiencing drastic labor imbalances.

Please remember this one point from this chapter - many more skilled trade jobs are available than there are high school students interested in taking those alternative career paths as they start their adult working years. This is a massive bonus for you as a high school student.

It means you plausibly could graduate high school and start working the next day in a skilled trade - and leave the tens of thousands of dollars behind that many of your peers will accrue during their four-year college days.

If you decide to enter a skilled trade, the day after you graduate from high school, you'll essentially be financially years ahead of many in your high school graduating class.

2

EXPLORING THE SKILLED TRADES

Your role in society is somewhat defined by your choices regarding your job and career, including the option to go to college or take a chance on an alternative career in the skilled trades. When discussing alternative careers, we're talking about those lucrative skilled trade jobs where you get paid for your work and skills, which helps businesses and industries thrive and profit.

You've got so many career paths to choose from – business, industry, teaching, research – each with different education requirements and job opportunities. It all depends on what the market needs and I assure you the job market is begging for skilled trade workers to fill some large holes left by those older folks who are retiring faster than replacement workers can fill their shoes.

Some jobs might only need basic schooling, while others call for specialized training from specific technical or trade schools. These actual skilled trades can set you up for success - both in your career and financially.

Skilled trade employment opportunities are divided into four main sectors: Primary, Secondary, Tertiary, and Quaternary, depending on the nature of the activities involved. Each sector encompasses distinct types of jobs falling under its umbrella.

In the Primary sector, jobs revolve around directly extracting raw materials from the environment. This includes mining, mineral extraction, farming, fishing, and more. On the other hand, the Secondary sector, commonly known as the Manufacturing sector, involves jobs related to processing or manufacturing products using those raw materials. So, jobs like producing steel or bread are prime examples of secondary sector jobs.

Moving on to the Tertiary sector, these jobs are all about providing services to people and other industries, which is why it's often referred to as the service sector. This sector encompasses various roles: broadcasting, hospitality, public health, telecommunications, transportation, nursing, and more. Finally, we have the Quaternary sector, which focuses on research and development and offers information-based services. For instance, jobs in Information Technology (IT) and Biotechnology research fall under the Quaternary sector.

If you seek a career with lasting job security and growth potential, look no further than skilled trades. Skilled trade jobs demand unique expertise, abilities, and knowledge, which students acquire through specialized training at apprenticeship schools, trade schools, or technical institutions. As a result, skilled trades offer a wide array of diverse career paths.

Opting for a skilled trade job presents a fantastic alternative to the conventional college-degree-required positions. These jobs equip you with industry-ready skills, ensuring competitive pay and high demand in various trades. Career opportunities within skilled trades fluctuate across different industries, contingent on the marketable skills acquired through top-notch professional trade school training.

TYPES OF SKILLED TRADE JOBS

As you get set to read the following few pages, I suggest you grab a pencil or a pen, as you might want to make some notes in this book if you read about a skilled trade that piques your interest!

As I explain to you the essential job duties of each skilled trade, I won't disclose the average pay rates for each trade. The US is a large country, and every state has skilled trades. When I researched the mean or median (average) pay rates for skilled trades workers, I felt it was subjective and inaccurate. Many factors play a part in determining the average pay for a professional trade worker, and there are considerably more factors in the US than I can list in this book. A skilled trade yearly income is regional and may have additional factors built in. Rest assured that I wouldn't be telling you that many of these skilled trades are six-figure careers if it weren't true, as there's a plethora of information on the web to validate my statement. Each state in the US is like its own smaller economy, so it's too difficult to arrive at an accurate average pay. It's safe to say that most skilled trades are upwards of a total package of USD $50 per working hour in pay and benefits.

Skilled trades encompass various job types across multiple sectors, focusing on Industrial & Energy, Technology, Construction, and Service. These jobs are typically divided into four main industry categories listed below.

Industrial & Energy Skilled Trades: Within this category, you'll find roles like welders, mechanics, machinists, tool and die makers, and even programmers. These professionals play crucial roles in industrial settings, contributing to the production and maintenance of machinery and technology.

Construction skilled trades: Jobs in this sector center around the residential and commercial construction industry and involve various trades essential to building projects. Carpenters, bricklayers, insulators, electricians, plumbers, and gasfitters are among the key roles in this category, contributing to the construction of buildings and infrastructure.

Service skilled trades: These trades are integral to the service sector, providing essential services in healthcare and related fields. The category includes roles such as nurses, orderlies, aides, therapists, and service technicians, all contributing to the well-being and support of individuals needing medical assistance.

Technology Skilled Trades: These trades form a critical part of the rapidly evolving technology sector, where professionals play essential roles in implementing, maintaining, and troubleshooting various technological systems and equipment. From network technicians ensuring seamless connectivity to telecommunications technicians keeping the lines of communication open, these skilled tradespeople keep our interconnected world running smoothly. Datacenter technicians safeguard the functioning of vast information repositories, while audiovisual technicians enhance communication and presentation experiences with advanced audio and visual solutions.

Additionally, computer repair technicians troubleshoot and fix hardware and software issues, contributing to the smooth operation of computers and devices. Cybersecurity specialists protect valuable data from digital threats, fortifying our technology infrastructure against malicious attacks. These and more technology-skilled trades are vital to the modern technological landscape, enabling businesses and individuals to thrive in an increasingly digital world.

INDUSTRIAL & ENERGY SKILLED TRADE EXAMPLES

Boilermaker: Boilermakers assemble, install, maintain, and repair boilers, closed vats, and other large vessels or containers that hold liquids and gases.

CNC Programmer: A CNC (computer numerically controlled) Programmer works with machinery that cuts raw materials into functional items. They are responsible for interpreting project blueprints, designing programs, and setting up machines to produce the components outlined in the program.

Electrical Power Line Technician: Electrical Power Line Technicians, or Lineworkers or Powerline Technicians, are skilled professionals responsible for installing, maintaining, and repairing electrical power lines and associated equipment.

Extraction Worker: As an extraction worker, you will play a crucial role in excavation by performing various essential job duties. You will be responsible for setting up and fine-tuning equipment and excavating geological materials. Additionally, your tasks will include preparing sites for excavation or boring, ensuring they are clean and ready for efficient operations. Working closely with extraction craft workers, such as earth drillers and derrick operators, you will provide valuable assistance during the extraction process. Your role will also involve signaling workers to commence geological material extraction or boring, ensuring seamless coordination on the site. Additionally, you will move equipment to transport materials and parts to excavation sites, contributing to the overall success and effectiveness of the extraction operations. Your attention to detail and commitment to safety will be vital in ensuring smooth and productive excavation processes.

Heavy Diesel Mechanic: A heavy diesel mechanic is a skilled trade professional responsible for maintaining, repairing, and servicing heavy-duty diesel-powered vehicles and equipment.

HVAC Mechanic: An HVAC Mechanic will install, repair, and maintain heating, ventilation, and air conditioning (HVAC) systems such as air conditioning units, rooftop air handling units, furnaces, boilers, and more.

Ironworker: Ironworkers fabricate, erect, hoist, install, repair, and service structural ironwork, precast concrete,

concrete reinforcing materials, curtain walls, ornamental iron, and other metals used in the construction of buildings, bridges, highways, dams, and other structures and equipment.

Mechanic: The role of a mechanic involves the upkeep and repair of cars, trucks, and other automobiles. Mechanics are tasked with inspecting vehicles to detect potential issues and subsequently addressing and fixing any problems they encounter. While many mechanics work on various cars, some specialize in a particular manufacturer or vehicle style to attain higher expertise in their field.

Millwright: A millwright is a skilled tradesperson specializing in installing, maintaining, and repairing machinery and equipment in various industrial settings. Their primary role involves assembling and aligning heavy machinery, such as conveyor systems, turbines, pumps, and manufacturing equipment, to ensure precise and efficient operation. Millwrights use various tools and techniques to fit and adjust machine parts, ensuring they work together seamlessly. They also perform regular inspections and preventive maintenance to identify and address any potential issues before they cause breakdowns or disruptions in production. Additionally, millwrights may be involved in troubleshooting and repairing mechanical problems to minimize downtime and maximize productivity. Their expertise in mechanical systems and machinery contributes to industrial operations' smooth functioning and reliability, making them essential assets in various manufacturing and production environments.

Pipefitter: A Pipefitter is a skilled trade expert in constructing pipe systems for heating, hot water, and cooling purposes. Additionally, they craft steam engines that power various types of machinery, such as dishwashers or clothes dryers. In their line of work, Pipefitters must be able to handle materials and tools such as large pipe fittings and welding machines. Pipefitters regularly install, replace, and repair natural gas pipes in all industries. Pipefitters regularly weld pipes and thus may also be considered steamfitters depending on their welding certifications.

Rotary Drill Operator: A rotary drill operator sets up or operates a variety of drills to remove underground oil and gas or remove core samples for testing during oil and gas exploration.

Solar Installer: The primary responsibility of a solar installer involves installing and maintaining solar panel systems. Apart from handling the installation process, a solar installer may also discuss solar options with property owners and ensure that all installations adhere to safety and local zoning regulations.

Steamfitter: Steamfitters are skilled trades workers who perform installations of pipes. They specialize in low to high-pressure steam pipe systems that allow liquids or gases to flow under high pressure. Their other duties include planning the layout of steam boiler rooms and steam piping systems and welding and fabricating the pipes carrying that steam. A steamfitter can also be a pipefitter; however, the welding certifications for the steamfitter differ.

Steelworker: A steelworker constructs steel frames, supports, columns, concrete reinforcements, and other steel structures. I-beams and steel columns are common work materials for steelworkers. They transport steel elements to the construction site, demarcate offloading and working areas, and prepare for installation by measuring, cutting, aligning, and placing steel structures. Steelworkers typically set the initial infrastructure that is the framework for many buildings.

Welder: As a welder, your primary role is to join metals using different welding techniques, such as MIG, TIG, Arc, or Flux-Cored Arc Welding. You'll work with metals like steel, aluminum, stainless steel, and cast iron, using your skills to connect them accurately.

Wind Turbine Technician: Wind turbine service technicians maintain and repair wind turbines.

CONSTRUCTION SKILLED TRADE EXAMPLES

Bricklayer: As a bricklayer in the construction industry, your primary duty is to install and repair brick and stone structures. You work with precision and expertise, interpreting architectural plans and blueprints to determine the layout and design of the project. Bricklayers skillfully prepare the work area, ensuring a level and stable foundation. They mix mortar and spread it evenly, placing bricks or stones in the desired pattern and aligning them accurately using various tools and techniques.

Carpenter: Carpenters are skilled craftsmen working with wood and other materials to construct and repair structures. Their job duties involve various hands-on tasks that require precision and expertise. Carpenters select and cut materials to size, ensuring they fit the design specifications accurately. They use tools and equipment, such as saws, drills, and hammers, to shape and assemble the pieces into the desired structures. Carpenters are skilled in carpentry, including framing, finishing, and cabinetry. In framing, they build the skeleton of a structure, such as walls, floors, and roofs, ensuring they are sturdy and level. Finish carpentry involves adding final touches to structures, like installing doors, windows, trim, and molding to enhance aesthetics and functionality.

Carpet Installer: Carpet installers are skilled professionals responsible for preparing the installation site, measuring, cutting, and laying carpets. They ensure proper adhesion using tack strips or adhesive, trim the carpet edges, and address any repairs or re-stretching needs. Carpet installers prioritize accuracy and customer satisfaction to deliver high-quality installations for residential and commercial spaces.

Cement Mason: As a cement mason in the skilled trade industry, your primary responsibility is to work with concrete to create durable and stable surfaces for construction projects. Your job duties include preparing the work area by cleaning and leveling the surface ensuring a smooth foundation for the concrete. You will then mix the concrete to the right consistency, using the appropriate proportions of cement, water, and aggregates. With careful precision, you pour and spread the concrete using tools like trowels, floats, and screeds to achieve the desired finish and texture.

Drafter: A drafter working in the skilled trade industry is vital in creating technical drawings and plans for various projects. Their duties involve interpreting design specifications and sketches provided by engineers and architects. Using computer-aided design (CAD) software, they meticulously transform these concepts into detailed and precise blueprints.

Electrician: Electricians in the skilled trade industry install, repair, and maintain electrical systems in residential, commercial, and industrial settings. You work with precision and expertise to ensure electricity's safe and efficient flow. Electricians begin by studying electrical blueprints and technical diagrams to understand the layout and specifications of the electrical systems. They skillfully install wiring, switches, outlets, and electrical panels, carefully following building codes and safety regulations. Your job duties also involve troubleshooting and diagnosing electrical issues, using specialized equipment and tools to identify and fix faults in electrical systems.

Fire Sprinkler Pipefitter: A fire sprinkler pipefitter is a skilled professional responsible for installing, inspecting, and maintaining fire sprinkler systems in buildings and structures. Their primary role involves working with a team to design and lay out the fire sprinkler system according to building codes and regulations. Fire sprinkler fitters then install pipes, valves, and other components of the system, ensuring it is interconnected and can effectively distribute water in the event of a fire. They perform tests to ensure the system's proper functioning and make necessary adjustments or repairs. Fire sprinkler fitters also conduct regular inspections and maintenance to ensure the system remains in good

working condition and is ready to respond in a fire emer
gency. Their fire sprinkler installation and maintenance
expertise is crucial in enhancing fire safety and protecting
lives and property from potential fire hazards.

Framer: A framer is responsible for constructing and assembling the structural framework (such as walls) of buildings
and other structures. Their duties involve reading and interpreting architectural plans and blueprints to determine the
precise measurements and specifications for framing
components. Using tools like saws, hammers, and nail guns,
framers cut and shape wooden or metal materials to fit the
specified dimensions. Framers also work with steel framing
members, resembling wooden framing members. They skillfully align and connect these components to create walls,
floors, and roofs, ensuring the structure is sturdy and level.

Glazer: A glazer is a skilled tradesperson who works with
glass and glass-related materials. Their primary role involves
cutting, fitting, and installing glass in various structures and
projects, such as windows, doors, mirrors, and glass parti-
tions. Glazers work with different types of glass, including
tempered, laminated, and stained glass, and they may also
handle glass repair and replacement tasks. They measure and
cut glass to precise dimensions, ensuring a proper fit, and
use various tools and techniques to secure glass panels in
frames or structures. Additionally, glazers may be involved
in sealing and weatherproofing glass installations to enhance
their durability and efficiency. Their expertise in working
with glass contributes to the aesthetic appeal and functionality of buildings and projects, providing a clear and trans-
parent element to architectural designs and interior spaces.

Laborer: A laborer is a versatile worker who performs various physical tasks and manual labor on construction sites, factories, and other settings. Their primary role involves assisting skilled workers and tradespeople in their functions, such as carrying materials, loading and unloading equipment, and operating simple hand tools. Laborers may be digging trenches, mixing concrete, laying bricks, or cleaning and preparing work areas. They play a critical support role, helping to ensure that construction projects and operations run smoothly and efficiently. Laborers are essential members of work crews, contributing their strength, agility, and adaptability to facilitate the completion of projects and ensure the overall success of various industrial and construction activities.

Landscaper: A landscaper is a skilled professional who designs, creates, and maintains outdoor spaces, such as gardens, lawns, parks, and commercial landscapes. Their primary role involves working with clients to understand their landscaping preferences and requirements and developing plans and designs to transform outdoor areas into aesthetically pleasing and functional spaces. Landscapers may plant trees, flowers, and shrubs, install irrigation systems, and lay down paths and walkways. They also take care of regular lawn maintenance, including mowing, trimming, and fertilizing, to ensure the health and beauty of green spaces. Additionally, landscapers may provide seasonal maintenance, such as leaf removal and snow clearing, and offer expertise in sustainable landscaping practices to promote eco-friendly and water-efficient outdoor environments. Their skills in creating and maintaining beautiful landscapes enhance residential and commercial properties' curb appeal and enjoyment.

Mechanical Insulator: As a mechanical insulator, your primary responsibility is to install insulation materials on mechanical systems, such as pipes, ducts, boilers, and tanks. You work to prevent heat loss, reduce energy consumption, and control temperature variations in commercial, industrial, and residential settings. Mechanical insulators meticulously measure and cut insulation materials to fit the specific dimensions of the mechanical systems. They skillfully apply insulation using various techniques, such as wrapping, taping, or sealing, to ensure a tight and secure fit.

Operator: An operator is a skilled professional who operates and controls heavy machinery and equipment used in various industries, such as construction, mining, and agriculture. Their primary role involves safely and efficiently operating machines like bobcats, tower cranes, boom cranes, backhoes, dump trucks, earthmovers, road grading equipment, and specific equipment to perform particular tasks, such as excavation, lifting, digging, or material handling. Operators are responsible for following safety protocols and guidelines, inspecting and maintaining their equipment, and ensuring that the machinery operates smoothly and accurately. They may work on construction sites, in manufacturing facilities, highway heavy projects, or in other outdoor environments, and their expertise in handling heavy machinery plays a crucial role in completing projects and tasks effectively and safely. An operator is commonly referred to as a forty-niner.

Operating Engineer: An operating engineer, or a stationary engineer, is a skilled professional responsible for operating, maintaining, and repairing various mechanical and electrical systems in buildings and industrial facilities. Their primary role involves monitoring and controlling equipment such as boilers, chillers, generators, and HVAC systems to ensure they function efficiently and safely. Operating engineers conduct routine inspections, perform preventive maintenance, and troubleshoot issues to prevent breakdowns and ensure smooth operation. They may also manage building automation systems and energy management, optimizing equipment performance and energy efficiency. Operating engineers play a crucial role in maintaining the functionality and safety of building systems, contributing to the overall comfort, productivity, and sustainability of the facilities they manage.

Painter: A painter's primary role is to apply paint and other finishes to surfaces, enhancing the appearance and protection of various structures. You begin by preparing the work area, which involves cleaning and sanding surfaces to ensure a smooth and even base for the paint. Painters skillfully mix paint colors to achieve the desired shades and tones specified in the project requirements. They carefully apply the paint using brushes, rollers, or spray equipment, ensuring consistent coverage and a professional finish.

Plumber: The primary responsibility of a plumber is to install, repair, and maintain plumbing systems in residential, commercial, and industrial buildings. You work with various pipes, fittings, and fixtures to ensure the proper flow and distribution of water and efficiently remove waste. Plumbers start by studying blueprints and technical diagrams to understand the layout and specifications of the plumbing systems. They skillfully install pipes, fittings, and fixtures, ensuring they are aligned, secure, and leak-free. Job duties of a Plumber also include troubleshooting and diagnosing plumbing issues using specialized equipment and tools to identify and fix leaks, clogs, or other problems in the plumbing system. Plumbers may work on various plumbing components, such as sinks, faucets, toilets, water heaters, and sewer lines, ensuring they work correctly.

Roofer: A roofer in the skilled trade industry is primarily responsible for installing and repairing roofs on residential, commercial, and industrial buildings. Depending on the project requirements, you work with various roofing materials, such as asphalt shingles, metal sheets, tiles, or membranes. Roofers prepare the roof surface, ensuring it is clean, level, and damage-free. They meticulously measure and cut roofing materials to fit the specific dimensions of the roof, ensuring a proper fit and tight seal. Using specialized tools and equipment, roofers skillfully apply roofing materials, such as nailing down shingles or securing metal sheets, to create a weatherproof and durable roof structure.

SERVICE SKILLED TRADE EXAMPLES

Cardiovascular Technician: A cardiovascular technician, also known as a cardiovascular technologist, is a healthcare professional who specializes in assisting with diagnostic and therapeutic procedures related to the cardiovascular system. Their primary role is to support cardiologists and other medical professionals in diagnosing and treating heart and blood vessel conditions.

Dental Hygienist: A dental hygienist is a licensed oral healthcare professional who promotes good oral hygiene and preventive dental care. Their primary responsibility is to work alongside dentists and dental teams to provide comprehensive dental care to patients.

Licensed Practical Nurse (LPN): A Licensed Practical Nurse (LPN) is a healthcare professional critical in providing direct patient care and assisting registered nurses and other health-care providers in various healthcare settings. The LPN's duties might include administering medications, dressing wounds, and recording patient statistics in medical charts and forms.

Medical Lab Technician: A Medical Laboratory Technician (MLT) is a healthcare professional who plays a crucial role in the medical laboratory setting. Their primary responsibility is performing various laboratory tests and procedures to diagnose, treat, and prevent diseases.

Physical Therapist: A Physical Therapist (PT) is a licensed healthcare professional specializing in providing rehabilita-tion services to individuals with physical disabilities or injuries. Their primary focus is to improve their patients' mobility, function, and overall quality of life. Physical thera-pists work in various settings, including hospitals, outpatient clinics, sports facilities, and home care settings.

Radiation Therapist: A radiation therapist administers radi-ation treatments to patients with cancer or other medical conditions requiring radiation therapy. Their primary role is to work as part of a radiation oncology team, which includes oncologists, medical physicists, and dosimetrists, to deliver precise and targeted radiation treatments to patients.

Registered Nurse: A registered nurse (RN) is a licensed healthcare professional who provides direct patient care and plays a central role in the healthcare team. Their scope of practice covers various responsibilities and duties across multiple healthcare settings, such as hospitals, clinics, nursing homes, and home healthcare.

Respiratory Therapist: A respiratory therapist specializes in providing care and treatments for patients with respiratory issues and breathing disorders. They work with patients of all ages, from newborns to the older generation, and often collaborate with other healthcare team members, including physicians, nurses, and respiratory therapy assistants.

Ultrasonographer: An ultrasonographer, also known as a diagnostic medical sonographer, is a healthcare professional specializing in performing ultrasound examinations. Ultrasonographers use high-frequency sound waves to create detailed images of internal body structures, such as organs, blood vessels, and developing fetuses during pregnancy. These images aid physicians in diagnosing and monitoring medical conditions and guiding medical procedures. Ultrasonographers work closely with patients to ensure their comfort and safety during the process, and they play a crucial role in providing valuable diagnostic information that helps healthcare providers make informed decisions about patient care.

TECHNOLOGY SKILLED TRADE EXAMPLES

Audiovisual Technician: An audiovisual technician is a skilled professional responsible for setting up, operating, and maintaining audiovisual equipment used in various events, presentations, and productions. Their primary role involves configuring sound systems, projectors, video displays, lighting, and other audiovisual equipment to ensure high-quality audio and visual experiences. Audiovisual technicians work closely with event organizers, performers, and presenters to understand their technical requirements and provide seamless support during events. They troubleshoot technical issues and make real-time adjustments to ensure the smooth flow of audio and visual elements. Additionally, audiovisual technicians may be involved in recording and editing audiovisual content, contributing to the production and distribution of multimedia materials. Their expertise in managing audiovisual technology enhances the overall impact and success of events, conferences, meetings, and performances across various industries.

Automation Technician: An Automation Technician is a skilled professional responsible for designing, installing, maintaining, and troubleshooting automated systems and machinery used in manufacturing and industrial processes. Their primary role involves programming and configuring control systems, such as programmable logic controllers (PLCs) and robotic systems, to automate tasks and optimize production processes. Automation Technicians perform regular inspections and preventive maintenance to ensure reliable and efficient operation of automated equipment. They collaborate with engineers and production teams to identify opportunities for process improvement and implement automation solutions that enhance productivity and reduce manual labor. Additionally, Automation Technicians diagnose and resolve technical issues in automated systems, minimizing downtime and maximizing overall efficiency.

Their expertise in automation technologies plays a crucial role in streamlining manufacturing operations and improving the performance and output of industrial processes.

CAD (Computer-Aided Design) Technician: A CAD (Computer-Aided Design) Technician is a skilled professional responsible for creating detailed technical drawings and digital designs using specialized CAD software. Their primary role involves translating concepts and ideas from engineers, architects, or designers into precise and accurate 2D or 3D drawings. CAD Technicians use their expertise to produce plans, blueprints, and models for various projects, such as architectural designs, mechanical components, electrical systems, and product prototypes. They work collaboratively with design teams to modify and update drawings, ensuring the final designs meet the required specifications and standards. CAD Technicians play a crucial role in the design and development process, enabling efficient and accurate visualization of complex projects and facilitating effective communication among project stakeholders.

Computer Repair Technician: The computer repair technician is a skilled professional responsible for diagnosing and resolving hardware and software issues in computers and other electronic devices. Their primary role involves troubleshooting computer problems reported by users or detected during diagnostic tests. Computer repair technicians disassemble and replace faulty components, such as motherboards, hard drives, memory modules, and graphic cards. They install and update software, including operating systems and applications, to ensure smooth system performance. Additionally, computer repair technicians provide technical support to users, offering guidance and instructions on resolving common issues and optimizing computer functionality. Their expertise in computer hardware and software enables them to restore and maintain the functionality of computers and electronic devices, ensuring users can work efficiently and effectively.

Cybersecurity Specialist: A Cybersecurity Specialist is a highly skilled professional responsible for protecting an organization's computer systems, networks, and data from cyber threats and attacks. Their primary role involves implementing security measures, such as firewalls, encryption, and intrusion detection systems, to safeguard against unauthorized access and data breaches. Cybersecurity Specialists conduct regular security assessments and vulnerability scans to identify potential weaknesses and develop strategies to mitigate risks. They monitor network traffic for suspicious activities and respond promptly to security incidents. Cybersecurity Specialists may hold certifications such as CompTIA Security+, Certified Information Systems Security Professional (CISSP), Certified Ethical Hacker (CEH), and Certified Information Security Manager (CISM), among others, to validate their expertise and knowledge in the field. Their expertise in cybersecurity ensures the confidentiality, integrity, and availability of an organization's sensitive information and technology assets.

Data Center Technician: A data center technician is a skilled professional responsible for installing, maintaining, and monitoring data center infrastructure and equipment. Their primary role involves setting up servers, networking devices, storage systems, and other critical components within the data center to support data storage and processing. Data center technicians perform regular inspections and preventive maintenance to ensure optimal performance and minimize downtime. They monitor data center operations, temperature, and power consumption to maintain a secure and efficient environment. In the event of technical issues or failures, data center technicians troubleshoot and resolve problems promptly, collaborating with other IT teams and vendors when necessary. Their expertise in managing data center resources and hardware ensures the availability and reliability of critical systems, supporting the continuous operation of IT services and applications for businesses and organizations.

HVAC Controls Technician: An HVAC Controls Technician is a skilled professional responsible for installing, configuring, and maintaining heating, ventilation, and air conditioning (HVAC) control systems. Their primary role involves setting up and programming control devices, such as thermostats, sensors, and automated building management systems, to regulate temperature, humidity, and air quality in commercial and residential buildings. HVAC control technicians perform system tests, diagnose malfunctions, and troubleshoot issues to ensure the efficient and optimal functioning of HVAC systems. They collaborate with HVAC technicians and engineers to integrate control systems into overall HVAC setups and provide technical support to customers regarding system operation and maintenance. Their expertise in HVAC control technologies contributes to energy efficiency, comfort, and cost savings in various indoor environments.

IT Support Specialist: An IT Support Specialist is a skilled professional responsible for providing technical assistance and support to end-users and organizations with their computer hardware, software, and network-related issues. Their primary role involves diagnosing and troubleshooting technical problems reported by users, guiding them through solutions, and resolving issues promptly to minimize downtime. IT Support Specialists assist with software installations, updates, system configurations, and setting up and maintaining computer networks. They may also provide user training on various applications and IT tools. Additionally, IT Support Specialists are vital in preserving cybersecurity, ensuring systems are protected against threats, and implementing security measures to safeguard data and sensitive information. Their expertise in IT support helps businesses and individuals to maintain smooth and efficient IT operations, enhancing productivity and ensuring the reliability of technology resources.

Network Technician: A network technician is a skilled professional responsible for installing, configuring, and maintaining organizational computer networks. Their primary role involves establishing network infrastructure to ensure reliable and secure data communication, including routers, switches, and access points. Network technicians troubleshoot and resolve network issues, such as connectivity problems or network performance slowdowns, and implement security measures to protect against unauthorized access and cyber threats. They also provide technical support to end-users, assisting with network-related problems and ensuring smooth network operation. Network technicians are crucial in maintaining efficient and secure organizational communication, contributing to the seamless flow of information and data across various departments and devices.

Penetration Tester: A penetration tester, also known as an ethical hacker or a white hat hacker, is a cybersecurity professional who simulates cyberattacks on computer systems, networks, and applications to identify vulnerabilities and weaknesses. The primary purpose of penetration testing is to assess the security posture of an organization's digital infrastructure and to find potential entry points that malicious hackers could exploit proactively. Penetration testers use manual and automated techniques to probe for security flaws, such as misconfigurations, software bugs, weak passwords, or other potential weaknesses that could lead to unauthorized access or data breaches. By conducting ethical hacking exercises, penetration testers help organizations discover and address these vulnerabilities before malicious hackers can exploit them, thereby improving the overall cybersecurity and resilience of the organization's digital assets. The results of penetration tests provide valuable insights that enable organizations to strengthen their defenses and enhance their ability to protect against cyber threats.

Renewable Energy Technician: A Renewable Energy Technician is a skilled trade professional installing, maintaining, and repairing renewable energy systems and technologies. Their primary role involves working with solar panels, wind turbines, geothermal systems, and other renewable energy equipment to harness clean and sustainable energy sources. Renewable Energy Technicians install and configure renewable energy systems to generate electricity or heat for residential, commercial, or industrial applications. They conduct regular inspections and performance evaluations to ensure optimal system efficiency and identify potential issues. In addition to installation, they also troubleshoot and repair renewable energy systems to maintain their functionality. Renewable Energy Technicians play a crucial role in promoting green energy solutions and reducing the reliance on non-renewable fossil fuels, contributing to a more sustainable and environmentally friendly future.

Robotics Technician: A Robotics Technician is responsible for the installation, maintenance, and repair of robotic systems used in various industries, such as manufacturing, healthcare, and logistics. Their primary role involves assembling and configuring robotic components, including mechanical parts, sensors, and control systems, to ensure the proper functioning of robots. Robotics Technicians program and test robots to perform specific tasks, collaborate with engineers to improve robot efficiency and safety, and troubleshoot technical issues to keep robotic systems operational. They also conduct regular inspections and preventive maintenance to identify and address potential problems before they escalate. Robotics Technicians are crucial in advancing automation and technology integration, contributing to increased productivity and precision in industrial processes and other applications where robots are utilized.

Telecommunications Technician: A Telecommunications Technician is a skilled professional responsible for installing, maintaining, and troubleshooting telecommunication systems and equipment. Their primary role involves setting up and configuring communication devices, such as phone systems, VoIP (Voice over Internet Protocol) systems, and data networks. Telecommunications Technicians perform tests and diagnostics to ensure proper functionality and resolve any connectivity or performance issues that may arise. They use various technologies, such as fiber optic cables, switches, routers, and wireless communication devices, to support efficient and reliable communication services. Additionally, they may collaborate with other IT professionals to integrate telecommunications systems into the overall network infrastructure of organizations, ensuring seamless and secure communication across different departments and locations. Telecommunications Technicians are vital in maintaining effective communication channels, contributing to businesses and institutions' smooth operation and connectivity.

ADDITIONAL UNCATEGORIZED SPECIALTY SKILLED TRADES

Air Traffic Controller: An air traffic controller is a highly skilled professional responsible for managing aircraft's safe and efficient movement within controlled airspace and on airport runways. Their primary role involves communicating with pilots providing them with instructions for take-offs, landings, and maneuvers to ensure the smooth flow of air traffic. Air traffic controllers use radar and other monitoring systems to track aircraft and maintain safe separation between planes, preventing potential collisions. They also coordinate aircraft movements with other air traffic controllers and ground personnel, such as ramp agents and baggage handlers, to ensure seamless airport operations. Additionally, air traffic controllers respond to emergencies and provide critical assistance during incidents or adverse weather conditions. Their expertise in managing airspace and coordinating aircraft movements is essential in maintaining the safety and efficiency of air travel, contributing to the overall success of the aviation industry.

Elevator Installer: An elevator installer is a skilled professional responsible for installing and maintaining elevators, escalators, and other vertical transportation systems in buildings and structures. Their primary role involves assembling elevator components, such as doors, rails, and control panels, and ensuring they are installed safely and in compliance with building codes and regulations. Elevator installers use their technical expertise to align and adjust equipment to ensure smooth and reliable operation. They may also conduct tests and inspections to verify that the elevator systems function correctly and meet safety standards. Additionally, elevator installers may perform maintenance and repair work to keep elevators in optimal working condition. Their expertise in installing and servicing vertical transportation systems contributes to the safety, accessibility, and convenience of buildings, enhancing the overall functionality and value of the properties they work on.

Interior Design: An interior designer creates functional and aesthetically pleasing indoor spaces. Their primary role involves working closely with clients to understand their preferences, needs, and budgets and developing design concepts and plans to transform interiors into attractive, livable environments. Interior designers select and arrange furniture, color schemes, lighting, and decorative elements to create harmonious and visually appealing spaces. They may also recommend materials, finishes, and accessories to complement the overall design theme. Additionally, interior designers collaborate with architects, contractors, and other professionals to ensure that designs are implemented successfully. Their expertise in space planning, design principles, and creativity allows them to create customized and unique interiors that reflect the personality and style of their clients while optimizing functionality and comfort.

MANY OPTIONS

As you've read, there are many options for a skilled trade career, and to be honest, I've only scratched the surface with this list. Many occupations fit the term "skilled trades," where a person needs to have specialized skills, knowledge, and expertise in a particular craft or role. Some skilled tradespeople create high-quality results or products and deliver services through skillful and artful workmanship. In contrast, other skilled trades provide technological innovation and keep our digital world running smoothly.

In contrast, other skilled trades take the care of our loved ones into their own hands and provide medical expertise in often fast-paced environments where seconds matter in life-and-death emergencies.

At the beginning of this book, I said that the term "skilled trade" is used loosely worldwide. Although every occupation in the world has specific job duties, meetings to attend, and problems that need an answer, skilled trades are no less important than a CEO position in a Fortune 500 company.

Yes, a skilled trade is somewhat of a singular term, but I assure you that every skilled trade listed in this chapter by no means is distinct by job duties. The primary descriptive job duties I've listed for the sixty-five-plus trades are just a snapshot of what each of these most sought-after trades offers. No two days are alike when working in a skilled trades occupation.

A plumber might be in a multi-million dollar mansion on one day, and the next day, that plumber might be working 10 feet below ground in a ditch attempting to repair a broken drain line. A penetration tester might try to break into a major retailer's website on a Monday and then have to fly across the country to break through a major airline's firewall on Friday.

A medical lab technician might be looking through a microscope to identify the next pandemic-type virus and, the next day, testing biological cells in a Petrie dish for possible advancement in the cure for cancer.

No two skilled trades are alike, so I suggest to you multiple times through this book to do additional research. If you're in the mindset that you don't want the crippling college loan debt that has risen to an overall value in the US of over 9 trillion dollars, consider the skilled trades as an alternative option.

I have talked to hundreds of skilled tradespeople, and nearly everyone is overly satisfied with their career choice. As much like myself, skilled tradespeople like variety. There is plenty of variety when working in the trades, as again, no two days are alike.

As we close out this chapter, I genuinely hope you took my suggestion at the beginning and highlighted or annotated the book if you found any of the trades interesting enough to do further research.

In the next chapter, we will talk about how it's possible to choose a skilled trade and gain the understanding that a skilled trade education is far less expensive than a typical four-year college program.

3

PATHWAYS TO SKILLED TRADES

APPRENTICESHIP

If you've previously read the second book in this series, *Apprenticeship Career Planning for Teens* (2023), you may find some similar information I wrote about in that book. If you haven't read that book yet, I strongly urge you to pick up a copy of the E-book for a comprehensive guide to researching, securing, and finding success in one of the hundreds of apprenticeships available in the US.

Apprenticeships play a vital role in training various skilled trades, offering a comprehensive learning experience for hands-on workers. Under the guidance of experienced journey-level tradespeople, apprentices acquire essential knowledge and skills while honing their craft. However, to achieve true mastery, mandatory classroom instruction becomes necessary. These classroom sessions cover critical topics, including job site safety, building codes, OSHA regulations, technical documentation, blueprints, and soft skills like communication, teamwork, and work ethic. This comprehensive guide provides valuable information for potential apprentices, such as the key industries that offer apprenticeships and the significant benefits of completing such programs. Additionally, it provides expert insights into the content and significance of apprentice training, underscoring its importance as a career development tool for skilled trades workers.

More than 27,000 formal registered apprenticeship programs exist in the U.S. as of 2022. According to the Department of Labor, there were nearly 615,000 registered apprentices in fiscal year 2022, including more than 205,000 new apprentices. The section below highlights some of the questions I've received about apprenticeships and the top industries for apprentices and includes critical insight into potential careers, job responsibilities, and much more.

What are Apprenticeships? Apprenticeships have a long history as a valuable training tool, dating back thousands of years. In ancient times, the Romans organized craftspeople into groups to uphold the standards and quality of their trades. Today, apprenticeships continue to play a crucial role in skill development. Apprentices work under the supervision of experienced journey-level craftspeople and receive payment for their work. However, besides practical experience, apprentices sometimes must attend unpaid classroom instruction (industry-specific). For instance, the curriculum for apprentices in the United Brotherhood of Carpenters and Joiners of America covers a wide range of topics, from print reading and hazardous materials to green building techniques, along with hands-on subjects like cutting stair treads and roofing rafters. Essentially, apprenticeships serve as a paid scholarship with a highly focused study in one subject, providing a valuable pathway to gaining expertise in a specific trade.

Are Apprenticeships Valuable? Apprenticeships are invaluable in ensuring a steady supply of skilled trades workers, just as they did in ancient times. These programs offer in-depth instruction in technical areas that may not be fully covered during the busy workday, providing apprentices with a well-rounded education. Additionally, apprenticeships contribute to increased retention rates, as reported by AmericanProgress.org. Apprentices tend to remain with companies that invest in their career development, fostering a strong sense of loyalty and commitment to their employers.

Who are Apprenticeships Meant For? Apprenticeships are designed for individuals new to a particular field and seeking to enhance their skills, increase their earning potential, and make valuable contributions in their job site or workplace. This work arrangement allows aspiring workers to learn a valuable trade while gaining practical experience in the field. Apprenticeships are open to both men and women, despite some traditionally male-dominated industries, such as ironworking, where apprenticeships are available to any gender that wishes to become a skilled tradesperson. To thrive in an apprenticeship, candidates should possess qualities like coachability, eagerness to learn, and a willingness to follow instructions closely.

What Should You Look for in an Apprenticeship? When considering apprenticeship programs, aspiring apprentices should prioritize opportunities for career advancement and higher pay as they progress in knowledge and skills. Look for programs that offer a balanced mix of hands-on learning and instruction from experienced professionals in the field. Additionally, some apprenticeship programs are affiliated with local community colleges and trade schools, providing additional educational resources and credentials, which can be advantageous when selecting the right apprenticeship opportunity.

Industries Needing Constant Supply Of Apprentices

Advanced Manufacturing. Advanced manufacturing comprises various industries, from producing batteries for Tesla's electric cars to milling high-strength fasteners for the aerospace sector. The industry offers diverse career paths, including CNC programming, machinist, tool and die making, and industrial maintenance and repair roles. CNC machine programmers are responsible for setting up computer-numeric-controlled machinery to create precise parts and tools. Apprenticeships in this field are commonly available through community colleges and vocational schools, often leading to an associate's degree. According to the Bureau of Labor Statistics (BLS), over 468,000 people were employed as machinists and tool and die makers in 2016, and the industry is projected to add 2,700 jobs through 2026. Median annual salaries for these roles were recorded at $67,480 in May 2020.

Automotive. The automotive industry revolves primarily around vehicle repair, offering career opportunities as automotive mechanics, automotive technicians, and diesel mechanics. In 2017, over 923,000 individuals were employed in repair and maintenance jobs. Diesel mechanics handle a wide range of diesel vehicles, from passenger cars and trucks to buses and large commercial trucks. Apprenticeship requirements vary, with some programs offered by diesel manufacturers. For example, the Cummins diesel apprenticeship program concludes with an Associate of Applied Science Degree. During training, apprentices earn at least 50 percent of journey-level wages and expect an average annual income of $46,360 upon completion. The field is projected to grow by 9 percent through 2026, offering promising prospects for those pursuing careers in the automotive sector.

Construction. The construction sector primarily involves new structures, residential homes, bridges, roadways, industrial plants, refineries, and more. As of 2018, the U.S. Bureau of Labor Statistics reported that over 7 million people were employed in construction jobs. Potential career options include carpenter, electrician, ironworker, plumber, Ironworker, and more.

The US construction industry is poised for substantial growth over the next decade, driven by a convergence of factors that create a favorable environment for expansion. One of the primary catalysts for this growth is the ongoing need for infrastructure development and improvement. Aging infrastructure and increasing demands for modernization and sustainability have spurred significant investment in roads, bridges, airports, and public transportation systems. Government initiatives such as the Bipartisan Infrastructure Law passed in 2021 allocate substantial funds for these projects, providing a robust pipeline of work for the construction sector.

Another crucial factor contributing to the growth of the US construction industry is the surge in residential and commercial construction. The COVID-19 pandemic accelerated remote work and e-commerce trends, leading to a rising demand for warehouse and distribution facilities, data centers, and other commercial spaces. Simultaneously, the desire for larger homes, coupled with historically low-interest rates, has driven a housing boom, increasing demand for residential construction. As cities continue to expand and suburban areas grow, the construction industry will likely see sustained demand for residential and commercial projects, creating a positive outlook for the sector over the next decade. Additionally, the industry's adoption of advanced technologies, such as Building Information Modeling (BIM) and sustainable building practices, will play a pivotal role in enhancing efficiency and sustainability, further propelling its growth in the coming years.

Estimating the median annual pay for a tradesperson in the construction industry is difficult due to the number of skilled trades working within the industry. It is safe to say, however, that skilled trade workers in the construction industry typically earn between $45 USD and $60 USD per hour of work. It's very plausible that skilled trade professionals working in the construction industry could easily attain a six-figure income.

Energy. The U.S. energy industry encompasses various sources, including oil, coal, natural gas, renewables, and others. This sector offers multiple job opportunities, such as solar photovoltaic installers, power plant and substation operators, wind turbine technicians, and power line maintenance and installation roles. Apprenticeships in the energy industry can vary depending on the specialty, typically spanning three to four years. For instance, line workers' apprenticeships combine on-site training with technical instruction in electricity, fiber optics, electronics, and other critical aspects of the field. Employment prospects for power line installers are projected to grow by 14 percent through 2026, and journey-level workers earned a median annual salary of just under $80,000 in May 2020.

Healthcare. Healthcare and its support operations significantly contribute to employment opportunities across the U.S. The industry encompasses a multitude of diverse jobs, including registered nurses, paramedics, pharmacy technicians, and nursing aides. Apprenticeships play a pivotal role in setting workers apart by providing training in cutting-edge technologies transforming the healthcare landscape, such as electronic health records. This training can lead to higher wages and increased career prospects. Renowned companies like CVS offer registered apprenticeships for pharmacy assistants, who primarily assist with order-taking and prescription filling at pharmacies. Employment for pharmacy technicians is projected to grow by 47,600 new positions (12 percent) through 2026, and pharmacy assistants earned a median annual salary of $49,750 in May 2020.

Hospitality. The hospitality industry encompasses food preparation and related occupations, including baker or pastry chef positions. As of 2018, the hospitality and leisure sector employed over 16 million people. Chefs and head cooks are vital in overseeing and preparing food at restaurants and similar establishments. Apprenticeships in this field are expected to last nearly 4,000 hours and typically take two years to complete. During their apprenticeship, individuals gain valuable insights into various aspects of the trade beyond the kitchen, including nutrition, beverage management, and leadership skills. Employment opportunities for chefs and head cooks are projected to increase by 10 percent through 2026, and their average salary was just under $56,000 in May 2020.

Apprenticeship Q & A

I'll summarize many initial questions and answers I receive when giving talks on apprenticeship to schools, community groups, and teen outreach programs. I share these presentations as a reminder to young adults and parents alike that options are available to enter the adult working world after high school. The summarized version of the talks I give is that young adult high school students may not know precisely what they want to do as a career when they graduate from high school, so why send them to college without even a semi-solid understanding of what life after college looks like?

That's where an apprenticeship can be very beneficial. Apprenticeships allow for a paid on the job training environment and provide the full education required to be successful in the specific occupation.

How long does it take to complete an apprenticeship? All apprenticeships vary in length. Most typically have a one to six-year commitment, which is entirely dependent on the apprenticeship industry. The US Department of Labor has a full explanation on its website of each registered apprenticeship in the US and the requirements needed to join that apprenticeship.

What happens if I decide to leave an apprenticeship and go to college? That's great! If you've been in an apprenticeship and realize that isn't the path you want to take, and you'd rather go to college, you can walk away from that apprenticeship with hopefully some skills you've learned that you can use throughout your lifetime! There is no commitment to staying in an apprenticeship, which is a choice, just like going to college. The only drawback of leaving an apprenticeship early is that you might be required to pay back some or all of the cost of your education if you were in an employer-sponsored apprenticeship program. An employer-sponsored program typically "sponsors" that apprentice and thus will pay some or all of the cost for that apprentice's education.

Do I qualify for an apprenticeship? You will qualify as long as you are eighteen years old when you'd like to start your apprenticeship. The US requires apprentices to be eighteen years old, have earned either a high school diploma or a GED (general education diploma), and depending on the industry in which you'd like to join an apprenticeship, you may need to have a background check completed which will determine whether a criminal record exists.

How long do I have to attend school as an apprentice? As per the US Department of Labor requirements, apprenticeships must have at least 144 classroom hours of training for each 2,000 hours of on-the-job training. As a comparison, a typical 4-year college requires between 120 and 180 credit hours of education to achieve a bachelor's degree. As you can understand - an apprenticeship education is a viable alternative to a college degree. A typical apprenticeship is a multi-year apprenticeship, so the reality is apprentices spend 144 hours a year in their classroom training, multiplied by the number of years of their apprenticeship. Is it safe to say an apprentice receives more career-focused education than an undergraduate degree seeker would get? It sure does!

How can I find and enroll in an apprenticeship program? Some apprenticeship seekers have sought career counselors or contacted local job placement programs in their communities. In my previous book, Apprenticeship Career Planning For Teens, I strongly urge young adults interested in apprenticeship to visit the United States website Apprenticeship.Gov as their starting point for finding local apprenticeships in their community.

To close out this sub-topic, I'll again stress that apprenticeships are the best avenue to start your skilled trades career. Nearly every industry provides apprenticeships, and almost every apprenticeship pays you in an earn-while-you-learn environment. This means you get paid to learn on the job while being trained by skilled and credentialed professionals who likely went through the same apprenticeship program you are now in.

Additionally, the education requirements for a skilled trades career path include only the curriculum you need to succeed in your occupation. This also means your education costs significantly less than a college bachelor's degree program. Most apprenticeships have a small nominal fee per year for your education. These fees typically are only forwarded to the apprentice as they may cover textbooks, a technology fee (some apprenticeships provide laptops or tablets), or the fee may be for hands-on consumable goods that you will use in your program (such as welding rod if you are in a welding apprenticeship or lumber if you are in a carpentry apprenticeship). Next, we will look at the career entry differences between vocational, technical, and trade schools.

POST-SECONDARY SCHOOL

Job seekers seeking training for lucrative careers may be confused by the various options available. The distinctions between trade school, vocational school, and tech school can be unclear, as the terms may vary in meaning across institutions or depending on the individual using them. Nevertheless, some differences can alleviate this confusion and guide individuals in choosing the right career training institution. Understanding these differences will help you decide which educational path is right for you and which will provide the best way to your future career.

Technical Schools. Technical schools, often called institutions, offering associate's degrees and specific certifications focus on preparing students for technical job fields. Unlike traditional four-year colleges and universities, these programs typically have a shorter duration, usually 1-2 years, and offer more affordable tuition options. Rather than spending time on broad "core curriculum" subjects, students directly study applied knowledge and skill development that aligns with their chosen career path.

Upon completing their technical education, students may still need to participate in training programs, apprenticeships, or entry-level positions to utilize their acquired skills fully. However, some associate's degrees and technical certifications allow graduates to start working immediately in their chosen field. Technical schools cater to those seeking a quicker and more focused route to career readiness, providing a viable option for individuals interested in pursuing specific technical professions.

Trade Schools. According to Merriam-Webster, trade schools, also known as "secondary schools teaching skilled trades," primarily focus on hands-on careers like auto mechanics, electricians, carpenters, and medical assistants. These industries often require a base-level certification or specific supervised on-the-job hours for entry. Trade schools offer more practical study programs than technical schools, where classroom lectures and simulated job training may be more common. However, it's worth noting that some trade schools teach tech school-style courses and have similar programs, blurring the distinction between the two.

Vocational Schools. Under the term "vocational school," institutions encompass trade and tech schools, where programs lead to specialized trade certifications or "vocational degrees." These vocational school programs aim to prepare students for immediate entry into their field or a stepping-stone position within just a year or two. While some four-year undergraduate institutions offer vocational degree programs, specific trades like carpentry may only be taught in vocational school settings.

The U.S. Department of Education may offer much-needed vocational training programs to public high school students, allowing them to swiftly enter a career after graduation, bypassing a four-year postsecondary academic institution. While public support for postsecondary vo-tech schools has diminished, private ownership of these schools has surged. However, vocational schools still utilize public programs like Federal Student Aid, enabling individuals to access job training and transition to new careers without significant financial barriers. Some vocational institutions have specialized trade training programs that offer certificates that prepare students for the workforce, positioning them as a true vocational institution or "vo-tech" school.

In today's fast-paced society, there is often confusion surrounding the differences between tech schools, trade schools, vocational schools, and other job training programs. These terms can be used interchangeably, and even the U.S. Bureau of Labor Statistics groups all instructors of these programs under the umbrella term "career and technical education" or CTE. Many people commonly refer to these career-focused schools as "vo-tech" institutions. Pursuing job training at a career-focused learning institution can be a wise choice regardless of terminology. Completion rates of four-year collegiate degree programs are only around 60% within six years, and rising tuitions have made individuals seek quicker graduation options that lead directly to job opportunities. Consequently, enrollment in vo-tech schools has increased. These schools offer flexible programs tailored to students' ideal career paths, featuring small class sizes and hands-on instruction to accommodate their busy lives.

When researching this topic, in hopes of providing you with a comprehensive list of "crossover" programs between vocational, technical, and trade schools, I realized that list could be long enough to be a book of its own. There are so many schools in the US that are classified as "vocational" (meaning most non-traditional college higher learning institutions) that the list could be a book in and of itself.

Financial Aid for Technical, Trade, or Vocational School

The term "scholarship" is commonly associated with four-year colleges, but it's important to note that this financial aid is not exclusive to traditional academic paths. Students pursuing skills-based training can also access numerous trade school scholarships and grants. Many local businesses and industries are keen on enhancing the pool of skilled talent and have established programs to assist students in financing their training. As a result, there are several vocational scholarships tailored to specific eligibility criteria. While researching and identifying suitable scholarships may require some effort, the payoff can be substantial. For the right individual, these trade school grants and scholarships open doors to a promising career path with a bright and rewarding future.

Financial aid for trade school is indeed available, and scholarships come from various sources, including the federal government, trade unions, and nonprofit organizations, similar to financial aid for community college.

Scholarship programs often have specific criteria, such as targeting particular fields of study or specific regions. For example, some Career and Technical Scholarships are designed to support vocational students in a particular state, thanks to contributions from local businesses and organizations. Exploring resources and programs available in your home state is essential if you're looking for financial aid or scholarship opportunities for trade school. You might discover local scholarships and funding options that align perfectly with your educational and career aspirations.

Students must complete the Free Application for Federal Student Aid (FAFSA) to kickstart getting financial aid for trade school. This crucial federal government form establishes eligibility for educational assistance, including grants, loans, and work-study programs. FAFSA information often plays a pivotal role in scholarship decisions, so filling it out is essential for scholarship applications.

Furthermore, FAFSA might lead to additional funding sources. However, it's important to remember that most federal student aid sources require trade school programs to be accredited.

Scholarships and grants can enable trade school students to graduate with minimal or no debt, which is a significant advantage compared to the average debt of around $10,000 USD faced by students attending four-year colleges, according to U.S. News and World Report.

If and when starting your research regarding a vocational school to skilled trades path, I strongly suggest you include the U.S. Department of Education Office of Career, Technical, and Adult Education information on their website. There is an extensive list of options for scholarships and grants.

Some category examples of available U.S. Department of Education grants and scholarships are:

- Grants and Programs While In High School
- Grants and Programs for Career and Technical Education
- Grants and Programs for Community Colleges

Many private companies, organizations, and individuals also provide vocational grants and scholarships to promote the skilled trades and help those who may not have access to financial aid for the non-traditional college path.

Many of these non-government affiliated companies provide their grant and scholarship information on a website called *College Consensus*, and a search of "trade school scholarships" on the website will bring you to a long list of available scholarships and grants for hands-on careers.

Here are some private organizations or companies that see the need for a rise in the interest in vocational schooling and occupations, and plausibly, these companies have felt the burden of not having enough representative workers to fill the open positions of the aging workforce nearing retirement.

- American Fire Sprinkler Association offers a scholarship for new apprentices into a fire and life safety apprenticeship.
- The Refrigeration School of Arizona offers scholarships to women interested in learning the refrigeration trade.
- Shear Comfort, a US leader in auto-seat cover production, offers scholarships for students wishing to learn Automotive Engineering or Auto Mechanics.
- The PHCC (Plumbing, Heating, and Cooling Contractors Association) offers yearly scholarships to promote women finding interest in the trades.
- The Merchants Exchange or Portland (Oregon) Scholarship Fund provides scholarships to students focusing on Maritime Affairs or International Trade.

Many websites are available to guide you toward scholarships and grants for hands-on trade apprenticeships. You should first search in your home community, then your home state, and then expand your search if needed.

With the significant US industries continuing to suffer a labor shortage, there are new approaches nearly every day towards finding the next generation of replacement skilled hands-on workers to fill the void. You certainly won't fall short when seeking your path into a skilled trade hands-on career. Suppose you choose that path through vocational, technical, or trade school instead of an apprenticeship by doing further research. In that case, you have an excellent opportunity to be given tuition help through scholarships or grants.

In the next chapter, we will start to identify and learn about the skills you will gain in the trades and skills you may already have that will help you in your hands-on career!

4

ESSENTIAL SKILLS FOR SUCCESS

THE ROAD TO MASTERY

Mastery of a subject or skill entails comprehensive knowledge, while comprehension means understanding all or nearly all aspects of something. Considering this definition, it becomes evident that achieving mastery in one's craft demands substantial time, effort, and determination. The fascinating part of attaining such expertise lies in the rewarding outcome it brings.

Embracing a career in skilled trades presents challenges and rewards, demanding a high level of expertise, skill, and dedication. While some may believe that becoming a master in a trade is solely a matter of inherent talent or luck, the truth is that it hinges on the power of consistent practice and refinement of knowledge and skills.

The significance of consistent practice and refinement on the career path to mastery cannot be overstated. Regular practice allows you to gain the proficiency, knowledge, and confidence necessary to excel in your chosen field. Additionally, embracing new technologies allows for exploring novel ideas and techniques, enhancing efficiency and effectiveness in work.

To highlight the impact of consistent practice and refinement, consider the story of John, a passionate carpenter. Struggling to find time to hone his skills, he eventually decided to dedicate himself entirely to mastering his craft. John witnessed remarkable progress through daily practice and the use of various techniques and tools. His projects were completed faster and more precisely, allowing him to undertake more complex tasks and acquire new skills.

Likewise, the journey of Mary, an experienced welder, exemplifies the power of consistent practice and refinement. By dedicating herself to refining her craft through regular training and innovative approaches, she observed significant improvements in her work. Mastering different welding techniques and utilizing various tools, Mary achieved greater accuracy and efficiency in crafting complex and detailed structures.

Last, we have Tom, a seasoned plumber, who echoes the same sentiment. He observed remarkable enhancements in his work after consistent practice and refining some of his methods. Learning new plumbing techniques and leveraging different tools enabled Tom to expedite projects while maintaining the high standards he set for himself.

The stories of John, Mary, and Tom serve as testimonials of the rewards of consistent practice and refinement in mastering a trade. These principles universally apply to any skilled trade, whether carpentry, welding, plumbing, or beyond. With regular practice and open-minded exploration, one can develop the skills, knowledge, and confidence to become an expert in their chosen field.

Supporting the significance of consistent practice and refinement is extensive research. Studies conducted by the American Psychological Association and the National Institute of Standards and Technology affirm that constant practice and refinement play vital roles in acquiring expertise. Devoting more time to these practices renders individuals more likely to achieve mastery in their respective fields. At the same time, those willing to experiment with new techniques observe notable enhancements in their work.

Consistent practice and refinement are pivotal to mastering any skilled trade. A person can cultivate the expertise and confidence needed to excel through diligent practice.

Additionally, refinement allows for exploring innovative ideas and techniques that enhance efficiency and effectiveness. By skillfully blending both elements, individuals can become masters of their craft and secure a prosperous future in skilled trades.

SKILL & ACHEIVEMENT

I read a book early on in my career as a skilled tradesperson, and the book was titled *Grit: The Power of Passion and Perseverance* (2018).

In this book, the social scientist and author Dr. Angela Duckworth explains that after fifteen years of studying and researching athletes, business professionals, and successful entrepreneurs and individuals from various fields, who devised a simple, theorized formula for achieving success. The condensed version of the theory is this:

Practice + Effort = Skill
Skill + Effort = Achievement

To elaborate on Dr. Duckworth's theory, the intensity of practice and effort directly impacts the level of skill acquired. Newly acquired skills coupled with continued and persistent effort will bring your achievements into view and likely feel like it wasn't difficult to achieve what you set out to do.

Imagine two children learning to shoot a basketball. While both may receive coaching on their technique, the child who practices more frequently and with greater dedication will progress faster in developing the required skills.

Dr. Duckworth's research emphasizes that skill acquisition and sustained intensity lead to remarkable achievements. As proficiency is attained in one area, one moves on to the next skill level, continuously repeating the process to improve.

Natural talent does not solely determine greatness; instead, it is passion, dedication, and determination that set high achievers apart. Mastery is a product of unwavering commitment, producing masters through continuous growth, not merely the development of inherent abilities.

You might be asking now, what does this have to do with the skilled trades or a hands-on career? Well, it has everything to do with a hands-on, skilled job. Many trades have two levels of recognized "mastery" within that trade. When apprentices graduate from an apprenticeship or enter a trade after completing their apprenticeship or vocational or technical school education, they are commonly known as "journey workers." This includes both men and women.

The highest level of acknowledgment a person can achieve within any given trade is known as a "master." Plumbers and electricians will take skills tests after completing the required time learning on the job and completing their apprenticeship school. Passing these initial skills tests will grant them the professional term journeyworker. If a plumber or electrician chooses, they can take a more complex, more involved skills and knowledge test that may earn them an additional credential stating that they have an expanded knowledge of their trade.

This knowledge in the case of a plumber might be related to having the ability to design a drainage system for a commercial building, or it may be that the plumber has an expanded knowledge of drinking water safety and how microorganisms affect a municipal water delivery system in a community. The plumber who passed the expanded skills test would now earn the designation of "Master" Plumber.

An electrician who successfully tested and passed a Master skills and knowledge test might have displayed that they understands the theory of electricity and how electricity affects a major metropolitan power grid, or maybe that electrician proves to be fully knowledgeable in rural versus populated power failures and blackout protection. Upon verification of that electrician's expanded knowledge and skillset, that electrician would now be called a "Master" Electrician.

The more you practice your craft daily on the job, the better you will become at it; there's no question about it. The more effort you give that practice, the more skills and knowledge you will acquire. You will achieve more when you continue exerting the same level of effort daily in a skilled trade career.

The one footnote I would add to Dr. Duckworth's theory above is that the more you achieve in your career, *the more valuable you become to an employer.* Bringing considerable value to an employer puts you in a perfect position. You likely will have more negotiating power for a raise if the opportunity comes up, or you might get to take on more responsibility and be a leader to the other workers.

Becoming a master of your craft is not solely related to skills or knowledge, however. There are other considerations that, although they might not categorically fit a term of skills or expertise, certainly play a part in nearly every working day of a skilled trade worker's occupation.

Below, I've listed eight additional things you can do as a skilled worker to get the most out of your career and achieve your desired success.

Develop your skills one at a time. To attain true mastery, perfect one skill at a time. Intensity is the key to unlocking your potential, as dividing your attention among various pursuits can hinder your progress. Avoid becoming a "jack of all trades and a master of none" by committing yourself wholeheartedly to mastering each skill individually. Embrace the power of focused dedication to propel your journey toward mastery and unlock your fullest potential.

Keep doing and practicing. While the desire to perfect one's craft is shared, the path to mastery often eludes many due to a lack of execution. The journey to becoming a master demands consistent and intense action. Avoid getting caught up in wishful thinking; instead, cultivate a habit of regular practice and dedicated time devoted to honing your skills. The bridge between aspiration and mastery is built with repeated, focused efforts. So, seize the moment and turn your dreams into reality through persistent action and unwavering commitment to your craft.

Rely on your peers. A caring and supportive network of parents, friends, coworkers, or a significant other can be a tremendous advantage on your path to mastery. Surround yourself with a close-knit group of individuals who genuinely care for you and have your back. They will uplift you when facing challenges and encourage you to focus on your goals. At the same time, they will keep you grounded and humble when you achieve success. With this intimate circle of support, you'll find the strength and motivation to overcome obstacles and reach new heights in your pursuit of mastery.

Set a goal and achieve that goal. Mastery is a continuous and never-ending journey. It embodies the essence of being a lifelong learner. Those committed to mastery understand that the process's plateaus and challenges are natural parts. On the other hand, those who merely dabble may give up when faced with obstacles. True masters, however, remain resolute and steadfast, embracing the long haul with unwavering determination. Their dedication to continuous growth and learning propels them on their never-ending quest for mastery.

Find a mentor or a coach. On the road to becoming good at something in your career, having a great coach or trainer who's been where you are and succeeded is like having a super helpful friend. They can enhance and encourage your path to success, pushing you to do even better. A mentor who has overcome the same challenges you're facing can give you beneficial advice and help you get better at what you're doing with their experience and knowledge.

Focus on your desire. Becoming good at something starts with wanting to be great, going above and beyond what's usual, and being excited about getting better. This strong desire keeps you on track, working hard, and eager to improve. Along with that desire, a solid commitment to success is like a strong foundation of a building for your career. It's a promise you make to yourself to stay determined, no matter the problems, and to keep going even when things get tough.

Take inspiration from around you. Learning about the careers of successful tradespeople in your career can boost your motivation. Start by digging into their stories and experiences to find one that aligns with your goals. Connect with them on LinkedIn for valuable advice and insights on their path to success. Let their stories of overcoming challenges inspire and motivate you to achieve your own goals.

Never stop learning or practicing. Becoming good at what you do begins with taking action, as the results you're looking for are most often discovered through learning by doing. Dive deep into focused practice and put all your effort into getting better. Staying consistent is super important, so whenever you go to work, give it your all daily. Don't fear tough challenges; see them as chances to learn and go beyond what you think you are capable of. If you keep at it with consistent dedication, your desire for perfection will take you to new skill levels, and you'll find yourself getting really good at what you do in your career.

ADDITIONAL UNREALIZED SKILLS

I also want to tell you about some often less thought-about skills that will help you in your skilled trade career. These skills aren't directly related to the hands-on work that a skilled tradesperson does often but are more of a self-aware set of skills that will help you along the way.

Expand your learning through curiosity. Staying open to new knowledge is crucial to do well in your personal and professional life. Whether running your own business or working for someone else, curiosity can lead you to try new ideas, think creatively, solve problems, and tackle difficult situations. Begin by asking "why" to uncover how and why things function as they do. This understanding gives you a better view of the situation, making it simpler to adjust to changes and grow confidently. So, stay curious, explore, and keep learning – the key to becoming more adaptable in a skilled trade career that's constantly changing.

Remain fluid and adapt. In my skilled trade career, I've understood the importance of having career fluidity and flexibility. It's not just about mastering and sticking to a single skill; it's about adapting to the industry's evolving landscape. Being open to learning new techniques and technologies is essential. As a tradesperson, I've realized that the tools and methods I use today may not be the same in a few years. Therefore, I've made it a point to continually update my skill set, whether it's through additional training, certifications, or simply staying informed about industry trends.

Additionally, staying flexible in my career has allowed me to explore various avenues within my field. I've taken on different roles and responsibilities, from apprentice to supervisor and then to project management. This flexibility has kept my work exciting and challenging, providing me with a broader perspective on the industry as a whole. It's allowed me to adapt to different projects and situations, making me a more valuable asset to my employers and clients. In the world of skilled trades, pivoting and remaining adaptable is not just a career strategy; it's a critical element of long-term success.

Get it done. You might find it challenging to adapt to change in many situations because you hesitate to take action. Maybe the task feels overwhelming, and you spend much time thinking about it instead of doing it. Waiting for the perfect moment can become an excuse, even though that ideal moment may never come. The desire for everything to be just right can lead to delays that aren't necessary. But in reality, taking action is the key to becoming more adaptable.

It's important to strike the right balance between thinking things through and taking action to cultivate adaptability. When you feel about 80% ready, that's a good time to take that step. Try not to act solely on impulse, but don't wait forever for everything to be perfect. Your ability to make timely and effective decisions is a crucial part of being adaptable.

Appreciate missteps and failure. If you want to be adaptable, it's important not to be afraid of failure – in fact, you should be open to it and even celebrate it. When you fear failing, it can stop you from being curious, flexible, and taking action – all things you need to be adaptable.

When you succeed, you can help others by sharing what you've learned, like new skills or ways of doing things. But when you fail, you can offer more value by sharing what didn't work. Embracing failure means you can gain knowledge and help make things work better. Through failure, you learn and get better at what you do. Finding small successes amid bigger failures is essential because this enables you to adapt and do better in the future.

Additionally, being adaptable isn't about predicting the future. It's about being aware of what's happening around you, staying curious and flexible, noticing when things change, and then doing something to improve things. When you intentionally embrace adaptability, you can improve your life and organization at handling challenges and ultimately achieve more success.

There could be an exhaustive list of skills needed that a young adult like yourself might consider they need in advance to have a long and successful career in a skilled trade occupation. I assure you that is about as far from the truth as possible.

As a high school student considering your options for what you're going to do starting the day after your commencement from high school, do you even know what all of your skills are yet? I don't think so (no offense intended), as the school system you just graduated from scratched only the surface of the skills you needed to be successful in that high school learning environment.

You may have been laser-focused in school, but many people are. But what were you laser-focused on? High school-related tasks and situations? Probably. When you're out in the adult working world, life has a much different landscape than the educational system you just graduated from.

As we move on from this chapter, I will reiterate that when you enter into a skilled trade occupation, the assumption is you'll be starting in a field you have zero knowledge of. If you're starting an apprenticeship or have done one or two years of technical school, you might have the education for that specific occupation but lack the hands-on experience. The reverse could also be true; whereas you've worked a year or two within a trade as a helper, you've decided that trade is an excellent fit for you. Now, you want to commit by obtaining the classroom instruction required to one day be recognized as a fully trained skilled worker in that field.

The path you choose to the trades is your own to decide, and you'll have to weigh the pros and cons of each path as I've described it to see what works best for you. However, I can assure you that the end result will be well worth whichever route you take into a trade.

Skilled trades have been around for centuries. If you think about the plethora of cathedrals in the world and the sheer amount of marble statues and stone work within those cathedrals, those "stone masons" who crafted those statues and chiseled every block represent a "skilled trade" from hundreds of years ago.

In the next chapter, we will discover how to thrive in the skilled trades through career advancement, entrepreneurship, and having an excellent work-life balance.

Be the Inspiration for Another Young Skilled Tradesperson!

"Choose a job you love, and you will never have to work a day in your life." –Confucius

Ask yourself this question: How much has your school taught you about skilled trades? I'd venture a guess that the answer is "not much" – if anything.

Don't get me wrong, there's a ton of useful knowledge you're getting from high school, but the sad truth is that, for the most part, the focus is on academic success and not the full range of possibilities there are out there for you once you leave school.

Vocational careers set you up with a trade for life – and a decent, stable pay packet to boot. But how are you meant to access that future unless you're given the information you need to get started? By sharing my own experience with you and making sure you have all the information you need to develop your own skills and find your calling, I aim to make sure you have a solid foundation to build on.

There are tons of teenagers like you out there who need this foundation, and I'd like to ask for your help in making sure they get it. Don't worry – it'll take you less than three minutes, and you don't even need to leave the house!

Spreading this essential guidance is as simple as leaving a short review online.

By leaving a review of this book on Amazon, you'll make sure other young people find it and discover the full range of possibilities in their future.

It really is that simple – reviews are how we find the resources we're looking for, and just a few sentences from you can have a real impact. You know how difficult it is to find information about a career in the skilled trades when you're in high school, so there really is no better person to do this.

Thank you for your support. Now, let's continue on, shall we?

5

THRIVING AS A SKILLED TRADESPERSON

The skilled trades can be an excellent choice if you're seeking a career path with growth potential. Unlike some higher-level positions that demand traditional academic qualifications, the skilled trades offer numerous opportunities for advancement within the field.

There's ample room for newcomers to grow and progress in the trades. Embarking on apprenticeships allows you to learn from seasoned professionals while earning a wage. These apprenticeships provide invaluable experience and often lead to certifications or licenses that can propel your career forward.

As you accumulate more experience, you become eligible for promotions within your company or even transition to another company within the same industry. You can unlock even more job prospects by pursuing additional qualifications and certifications. Plus, the skills you acquire in the trades can be transferable to other industries, enabling you to explore new career avenues if desired.

The possibilities are boundless for those committed to a life-long trades career. Building years of experience and establishing a solid reputation in the field can pave the way for career advancement or even launching your own successful business. With the right mindset and dedication, you can rapidly progress from an apprentice to an expert in your chosen field.

I've given you the bullet points and highlights of my career in the introduction to this book, and my career highlights are not all that irregular, meaning anyone in a trade who desires to succeed and pushes themselves out of their comfort zone can and will be successful.

A skilled tradesperson can quickly achieve a natural career progression to any of these typical skilled trade positions, which are not in any given order, nor is this an exhaustive list of the positions that trade workers could achieve.

Foreman/Forewoman. A Foreman/Forewoman is a professional tradesperson who shows responsibility, motivates others, and proves they have abilities and skills beyond their daily work requirements. They work closely with managers to determine hiring needs, deadlines for specific tasks, and safety protocols to enforce among workers. They host meetings on-site and use their trade experience in this role, depending upon what's needed most within an industry setting.

General Foreperson/Superintendent. Plans, schedules, assigns, and supervises the work of journey-level workers of various building trades involving construction, maintenance, alteration, and repair of buildings and equipment.

Regularly reviews on-site work in progress for adherence to job specifications, building and safety codes, and project timelines. A general foreperson will communicate between the field and project management staff, ensuring a project progresses in a timely manner.

Shop Foreperson. A shop foreperson manages the staff delegated to the specific machine, production, or tool shop they control. The shop foreperson creates all work details for equipment and tool maintenance and creates employee work schedules. The shop foreperson also addresses factors that impede operations. Enforces safety regulations and protocols and conducts performance reviews with staff.

Responsible Individual. A responsible individual provides trade credentials and licenses to an employer and assumes the professional responsibility required for a company that conducts business in a particular industry. The responsible individual is typically a Master level worker and is the point of contact for workmanship disputes should those arise. The responsible individual could receive a higher wage or additional benefits beyond their regular pay rate in exchange for using their credentials or license to the company.

Project Manager. A project manager with estimating responsibilities is crucial in overseeing construction projects from start to finish. Their duties encompass a wide range of tasks that involve planning, coordinating, and executing various aspects of the construction process. Project managers are often involved in project planning, such as milestone completion dates. Project managers are

heavily involved in the cost estimation of projects and typically are responsible for overseeing the project budget and
project revenue. Project managers also must be keenly
aware of project risk management and how to mitigate situations that may prove costly to the expected revenue of a
project or, alternately, may affect a project schedule, which
could have a negative financial impact on a project. Not all
project managers are skilled tradespeople. If you ever want
to work on the project management side in your occupation, having hands-on field experience is very beneficial
over a non-trades project manager.

CAD Designer. In a previous chapter, I gave you a lengthy
description of a CAD designer's job duties, so I'll give you a
quick refresher. A CAD designer typically sits at a computer
terminal creating what will eventually become blueprints,
product diagrams, schematic drawings for fluid systems or
electrical circuits, or a host of other technical drawings.
These technical drawings can be two- and three-dimensional, and the recipients of a CAD designer's work will rely
on those 2D or 3D drawings to complete their tasks for that
project. A CAD designer is crucial to the construction,
manufacturing, and engineering industries. Computer-
aided Aided Drafting is constantly evolving into better
methods and software. CAD will be a very valued skill in the
next few decades as much of the US infrastructure is
nearing the end of its useable life cycle.

Business Owner. It is not uncommon for a skilled tradesperson to become a business owner one day. (I was a skilled
trade business owner, as I told you in the Introduction).
People worldwide dream of owning their own businesses,

and it takes a specific type of person to act upon those dreams and make them happen. As a skilled tradesperson, a vision of owning your own business one day is probably closer to reality than you could imagine. If you are in a hands-on career (as most trades are) and are working for a company that sends you to different locations or job sites to do your work, that company generates revenue from your education, skills, and skilled labor. At the end of the week, they'll pay you for your work, and that scenario happens week after week. You might decide one week that you want to generate your revenue and keep all the money your company makes from your work, and you decide to start your own business. Anyone can become a business owner who chooses to; you just need to make your attempt. Different companies have different risk factors, and if you are a skilled tradesperson setting out on your own, your risk factor is pretty low. Independent owners of hands-on skilled trade companies can fully support themselves and have a lucrative self-employed career for years. It takes a bit of business acumen to understand the day-to-day of running your own business, but many people say it's very well worth the work and the minimal risk as a skilled trade business.

Inspector (State or Municipal). A state or municipal skilled trades inspector is a professional responsible for ensuring that construction projects and building structures within their jurisdiction comply with relevant building codes, safety regulations, and industry standards. These inspectors are critical in safeguarding public safety and ensuring construction activities meet code-established requirements. An inspector might look at HVAC one day and the next visit a different location to see if windows were installed according to the local codes. Inspectors must constantly review blueprints for future projects and provide feedback and regulatory references if those blueprints do not meet the code. An inspector must have good communication skills, as they are not just solely interacting with construction or manufacturing professionals; they also have to meet with members of a community as a homeowner might need guidance on a home project if the inspector determined that the homeowners' project does not meet applicable codes. Inspectors are often skilled tradespeople who have spent many years in a hands-on position and attained their Skill and Achievement goals, which Dr. Angela Duckworth discussed in Chapter 4.

These eight career positions I've given you are only a snapshot of what additional options some industries offer for a skilled trade worker. There are more positions than I've listed, and some may be industry-specific. For example, in the Energy industry, you might see super tall electrical towers holding miles-long electrical cables very high up in the air attached to the tops of these tall towers. Have you ever wondered how those cables make it up to the tops of those towers when there isn't a ladder a person can use to get up there and secure the wires? *Helicopters, that's how.* Somewhere, someone's job is to schedule helicopters to hover over these enormous electrical towers and place those cables into some attachment on the top of the tower. Additionally, those cables are sometimes miles long and stretch from tower to tower, and it's someone's job to manage those tasks being performed by the helicopter company. The person who does that job likely got their start in a skilled trade career.

There are many options that skilled tradesperson has to advance their career. Defining what your "career advancement" looks like is something you will want to do when you start your hands-on career.

SKILLED TRADES INCOME

There are two income scenarios for a skilled tradesperson, and if you decide on the skilled trade route for your career, you'll have to choose which one you would like to pursue. I won't go into too much detail about the two different scenarios, as I've explained them in the second book of this series, *Apprenticeship Career Planning For Teens (SugarDog Publishing, 2023).*

In short, the two income scenarios are a salaried worker as a skilled tradesperson or an hourly paid employee as a skilled tradesperson. I'll provide you with some of the talking points I gave in the Apprenticeship Career Planning For Teens book and summarize those talking points.

Salaried Skilled Tradesperson. The pay structure for a salaried skilled tradesperson is designed to compensate individuals based on a fixed amount per week, month, or year. This scenario can benefit both the employee and the employer, as it offers flexibility for the employee and a known salary amount to the employer regardless of the hours a skilled trade employee works.

Here's an explanation of the pay structure and options for a salaried tradesperson:

Fixed Salary: Salaried skilled tradespeople receive a fixed, regular payment from their employer. This payment is typically based on an annual or monthly basis and remains consistent regardless of the number of hours worked in a given week.

Base Salary: The base salary serves as the foundation of the compensation package; it reflects the core value of the individual's skills and experience in the trade. Often, the base salary is accompanied by a performance-based commission bonus or a profit-sharing program if available through an employer.

Overtime Compensation: Depending on the job requirements, salaried tradespeople may be eligible for overtime pay. As is typical whether in a skilled trade occupation or any other occupation, a salary pay structure doesn't normally allow for additional pay beyond regular working hours. However, working as a salaried skilled tradesperson certainly allows you to negotiate overtime pay with your employer.

Benefits and Perks: Many salaried positions in the skilled trades come with additional benefits and perks. These may include health insurance, retirement plans, paid time off, bonuses, and other incentives. These benefits contribute to the overall value of the compensation package.

Skill and Experience: Their salary can increase as skilled tradespeople gain more experience and expertise. This progression may be based on a predetermined schedule or performance evaluations.

Promotions and Advancement: Advancement within the trade can lead to higher-paying positions. For instance, an electrician who is a supervisor may earn a higher salary than a journeyman electrician.

Union and Industry Standards: Some trades are heavily unionized, and union agreements determine their pay structures. These agreements outline minimum wages, benefits, and other compensation-related factors.

Cost of Living and Location: The geographic location can also impact a skilled tradesperson's salary. Areas with higher living costs often offer higher wages to offset the increased expenses.

Industry Demand: The demand for certain trades can influence salaries. Shortages in specific skilled trades may lead to increased compensation to attract and retain talent.

Education and Certification: Specialized education, training, and certifications can also contribute to salary levels. Individuals with advanced certifications or specialized skills may command higher pay.

Additionally, a salaried skilled tradesperson's pay structure encompasses a fixed base salary, potential overtime compensation, benefits, and opportunities for advancement. The salary can be influenced by experience, location, industry demand, and education. The compensation package aims to recognize the individual's expertise and contributions to the trade.

Hourly Skilled Tradesperson. The pay structure for an hourly skilled tradesperson is designed to compensate individuals based on the actual hours worked. This approach is common in many skilled trade industries and links the hours worked and the earnings received.

Here's an explanation of the pay structure and options for an hourly-paid tradesperson:

Hourly Wage. Skilled tradespeople who are paid hourly receive a predetermined wage for each work hour. This wage is usually negotiated or set by the employer based on factors such as the job's complexity, the individual's skill level, the industry standards, and the geographic location.

Regular and Overtime Hours. The workweek for hourly tradespeople typically consists of normal hours and potential overtime hours. Regular hours are the standard working hours defined by the employer, while overtime hours are any hours worked beyond the regular hours. Overtime pay is often higher than the average hourly wage and is mandated by labor laws in many regions.

Overtime Compensation. Overtime pay is intended to compensate workers for the additional time they put in beyond the standard workweek. In many cases, the overtime pay rate is 1.5 times the regular hourly wage, but this can vary based on local laws and collective bargaining agreements.

Shift Differentials. Some skilled trades require work during non-traditional hours, such as nights or weekends.

In such cases, employers may offer shift differentials, which are higher hourly rates for working during these less desirable shifts.

Piecework and Production Bonuses. In specific trades, workers are compensated based on the quantity of work completed. This is known as piecework. In addition, some trades offer production bonuses, where workers earn extra pay for exceeding production targets.

Benefits and Perks. While hourly workers may not receive the same benefits as salaried employees, most hourly skilled trade workers are provided with health care insurance, retirement plan contributions, and other benefits.

Skill-Based Pay Increases. As skilled tradespeople gain experience and improve their skills, they may be eligible for pay increases. These increases can be tied to achieving certain milestones or demonstrating proficiency in specific tasks.

Union Agreements. Many skilled trades are unionized, and unions negotiate their members' pay rates, working conditions, and other benefits. Union agreements often provide standardized pay scales and guidelines for wage progression.

Career Advancement. Advancing within a skilled trade can lead to higher hourly wages. For example, an apprentice progressing to a journeyman or a journeyman becoming a master may result in increased hourly pay.

Local and Industry Factors. The local cost of living, demand for specific trades, and industry standards can all impact the hourly wage offered to skilled tradespeople.

To reiterate some of the talking points above, hourly-paid skilled tradespeople receive compensation based on their work hours, with regular and overtime hours factored into their earnings. Hourly wages, overtime pay rates, benefits, and career progression opportunities vary based on skill level, industry, geographic location, and employment terms. The pay structure is designed to fairly compensate individuals for their expertise and the time they dedicate to their trade.

AVERAGE INCOME POTENTIAL

As a high school student thinking about alternative options to college (you're reading this book, after all), you'll probably want to have at least a general idea of some of the more popular skilled trades compensation packages.

The US Bureau of Labor and Statistics (BLS) regularly publishes mean/median salary rates in their Occupational Outlook Handbook publication. I highly recommend you further your research into which skilled trades interest you the most by visiting their website and simply entering "apprenticeship" in the search bar on the homepage. The US Bureau of Labor and Statistics has an extensive database of skilled trades occupations and average compensation rates. "Average" compensation rates are a bit subjective, however. As I've said a few times in this book, average pay, whether salaries or hourly wage, depends on which region of the US you are in and the industry's market share where you will be a skilled tradesperson.

Union representation in the skilled trades plays a factor in the mean/median compensation rates, so you'll also have to consider that. Typically, a union skilled trades occupation pays a certain percentage over what a non-union skilled trades position pays. However, a non-union skilled trades job might have better benefits for vacations, paid holidays, or child care reimbursement during the work day.

Below is a list of 24 skilled trades that rank at the top of the BLS statistics for best-paying skilled trades jobs as of 2021. These numbers are subjective and are only an average base guideline for information seekers like yourself considering a skilled trades career. I would recommend using these mean/median numbers as the low end of what these skilled trades pay.

This list is in alphabetical order, not from highest pay to least. The trade job title is listed first, with the median yearly income per year (excluding benefits) following the job title.

- Aircraft technician $65,550 per year
- Automotive service technician $46,880 per year
- Boilermaker $64,290 per year
- Cable technician $60,370 per year
- Computer support specialist $57,910 per year
- Construction inspector $61,640 per year
- Dental hygienist $77,810 per year
- Diagnostic medical sonographer $75,380 per year
- Electrical lineman $74,530 per year
- Electrician $60,040 per year

- Electronics engineering technician $63,640 per year
- Elevator mechanic $97,860 per year
- HVAC technician $48,630 per year
- Ironworker $57,160 per year
- Licensed practical nurse $48,070 per year
- Radiation therapist $82,790 per year
- Respiratory therapist $61,830 per year
- Nuclear medicine technician $78,760 per year
- Millwright $59,380 per year
- Paralegal $56,230 per year
- Plumber $68,380 per year
- Pipefitter $59,880 per year
- Power plant operator $94,790 per year
- Real estate agent $48,770 per year
- Solar energy system installer $47,670 per year

As you can see from this aggregate list extracted from the BLS website, the average yearly pay for some of these skilled trades is nearly six figures, and that's at the subjective rate with additional factors built into those dollars per year.

The US Bureau of Labor and Statistics website is an invaluable resource for alternative career path seekers. It gives US data on many hands-on skilled trade careers in many industries starving for a replacement workforce for hands-on positions.

Without question, a high school student like yourself can easily transition from high school into a skilled trade where, in typically less time than it takes to earn a four-year bachelor's degree, you could already be tens of thousands of dollars ahead of your peers simply by deciding to pursue a career in the trades.

BALANCING WORK & LIFE IN THE TRADES

The shortage of workers is making it tough to find enough skilled tradespeople for jobs in many industries. This means workers might have to do more work, and that can lead to feeling more stressed. On top of their jobs, they have other things to do, like taking care of their families and handling money matters. Taking care of their health and feeling good might not be a top priority.

It's a tricky balancing act between work and the rest of life. This balance is called work-life balance. You might have heard this term, but have you considered its meaning? It's about figuring out how much time you spend working compared to spending time with your family and doing things you enjoy.

Why is this balance so important? Not having a good balance between work and life can harm your health. If workers are struggling mentally, it can show in how they work. They might miss workdays, have accidents on the job, not get along with coworkers, or feel tired and stressed out.

The pandemic of 2021 certainly made things even harder. Working hard during the pandemic to support families plausibly has caused stress and mental health problems worse for important skilled workers. Many "essential" industries seemed to not skip a beat during the pandemic due to the US Government's designation that essential workers should keep working. Many tradespeople appreciated that their jobs were not lost during the pandemic, while other industries, private businesses, and small businesses shut down as directed.

Since the end of the pandemic, I've talked to many skilled workers about how they survived as a family unit when the shutdown occurred, and many of those people told me that although their partner or spouse might be delegated to work from home, it seemed that it was an excellent opportunity to review their work-life balance.

During the COVID-19 pandemic, many governments and authorities designated specific trades and industries as "essential" to ensure critical services and infrastructure continued functioning. These essential trades were allowed to operate even during lockdowns and restrictions, as their work was considered vital for public health, safety, and maintaining essential services. The list below of essential trades delegated to continue working throughout the pandemic could vary by state and region of the US. Still, generally, the following types of trades were commonly considered essential during the pandemic:

Healthcare Workers: Healthcare professionals, including doctors, nurses, paramedics, and medical support staff, were at the forefront of the pandemic response, providing medical care, testing, and treatment for COVID-19 patients.

Emergency Services: First responders, such as police officers, firefighters, and emergency medical technicians (EMTs), provided critical services to ensure public safety and respond to emergencies.

Utilities and Infrastructure: Workers in utilities like water, electricity, and natural gas, as well as those responsible for maintaining transportation infrastructure (roadways, bridges, and public transportation), were deemed essential to keep essential services running smoothly.

Construction Trades: Many construction trades were considered essential, especially those involved in building and maintaining healthcare facilities, emergency shelters, critical infrastructure, and public works projects.

Food and Agriculture: Workers in the food and agriculture sector, including farmers, food processors, distribution personnel, and grocery store employees, were essential to maintain the supply chain.

Manufacturing: Manufacturing industries producing essential goods like medical equipment, personal protective equipment (PPE), pharmaceuticals, and cleaning supplies were necessary to support the pandemic response.

Transportation: Transportation workers, including truck drivers, delivery personnel, airline staff, and transit workers, played a critical role in ensuring the movement of goods, medical supplies, and essential workers.

Waste Management: Waste collection and sanitation workers were essential to prevent public health hazards and maintain cleanliness during the pandemic.

Communications and Information Technology: Workers in the IT and telecommunications sectors were essential to maintain communication systems, internet services, and information flow.

Government Services: Government employees responsible for essential functions such as public health, safety, and emergency response continued to work to support the community.

It's important to note that the designation of essential trades could vary depending on the severity of the pandemic in a specific region and the decisions made by local authorities and governments. The goal was to balance protecting public health and safety while ensuring the continued operation of critical services.

As you can read from the list above, many industries where skilled trade workers are the lifeblood of the industry were given the green light to continue working during the pandemic as essential services are just that - *essential.*

These reasons should be a checkmark in your research that many trades perform functions daily that most of society cannot live without, and those trades are likely to survive future global chaos should that ever happen again, which we will hope a pandemic of that size and scale will never happen again.

Work-life balance is not just about the workers. Your company also feels the effects. How? Workers who are happy and healthy tend to do a better job and work more. Remember that worker shortage I keep mentioning? If employees do well and employers care about their health, they will likely stick with the company. And if they stay, the company won't have to spend nearly as much time finding replacement workers.

When you become a skilled tradesperson, you are the only one who can dictate what you need to balance your work life with your personal and home life.

When I was researching the work-life balance among most of the skilled trades I mentioned in a previous chapter, I was surprised that there isn't anything written by anyone specifically targeting work-life in the trades. I found it amusing that most of society thinks that office workers, whether in occupations like banking, sales, management, retail (etc.), struggle with finding the right work-life balance. What I never discovered was how the construction worker, or the truck driver, or the HVAC technician, or the registered nurse finds their balance between home and a demanding career that, although it pays very well, also has demands within that career that typical "white collar" professionals might not have in their office. The work-life balance differences between office workers and hands-on workers are drastically different and should be acknowledged as such in professional circles.

Among the many tradespeople I've conversed with about their work-life balance, many commented they either excelled at their balancing act or epically failed. However, finding a balance is not a one-time thing; it takes work and revisions. If something isn't working for you, change it up. Interruptions happen to that balance, and that's where the skill of fluidity that we've already talked about comes in. If you can remain open to changing aspects of that work-life balance on the fly, you will find success and happiness living a life as a skilled tradesperson.

Here are some responses I've received when talking to skilled workers about work-life balance through my vocational teaching.

Eat meals as a family. This seems so simple, but with the hustle and bustle of daily life, it often goes unmentioned when mom or dad throws a twenty on the counter and instructs the teenagers to have some food delivered. That's okay in extreme situations, but as a society, we quickly choose a convenient path over other things, and it happens all too much. Your days are never the same when working a hands-on skilled trade career. You might be at different work sites throughout the week and performing other tasks at each location. You might be working alone for an entire week and enjoy that, but you also might not like that. Working in a skilled trade sometimes means you're pulled in multiple directions multiple times a day. Hands-on occupations are arguably as much hand-on as they are hands-off due to regular distractions, and making a concerted effort to carve out purposeful family time by enjoying your nightly meal together will keep your distractions at bay when you get home and grounded in your roots as a family.

Additionally, you should feel less disconnected as a family if you ever need to miss that meal, as your job might require you to work overtime or even overnight. When my wife and I were raising our family, we made it a point to eat meals every night together with the kids. Those meals had one rule: no electronic devices on the table.

Take time for activities and hobbies - together. There's a typical saying for workers in skilled trades; it's not an original saying, but it is fitting. That saying is, "Work hard, Play hard." Skilled trades workers often work forty-plus hours a week, sometimes week after week and month after month. If you've never understood how much work there is to do when you're in some specific trades more than others, pay attention to the road construction projects in your home state. Where I live in the midwest, most residents comment that there's a harsh winter season, and then there's an even worse road construction season until winter comes back around.

It doesn't matter which industry you will be working in; a hands-on trade occupation will provide you 40 hours of work a week, year after year. Those 40 weekly hours could likely grow to a more significant number at some point. You will work hard in the trades; that's what the "blue collar" in blue-collar work is. Work hard during the week, and take your weekends off for family, hobbies, or whatever else you like to do when you have two days of no work ahead of you. Incorporating your partner, spouse, or kids into your hobbies will solidify your decompression time from the job requirements during the week. In my quarter-century-plus career in the trades, I made every attempt to spend time with my spouse and kids on the weekends doing things we all liked to do together. It wasn't necessarily my hobbies, as some of my hobbies my spouse or my kids just weren't interested in, and that was acceptable, as we found other things we enjoyed doing as a family. Did I compromise my enjoyment of doing my hobbies through these years? Maybe, maybe not. What matters is the time we spent together when I wasn't working 50-60 hours a week and trying to sneak in family meals and activities we could do together. I'll have time to return to my hobbies when I retire, and I'm guessing my kids will join me then.

It's acceptable to say NO. Skilled tradespeople naturally are a hit at a party, and everyone wants your phone number as they have a "side job" for you to do. I've been called by people with six degrees of separation from me because they heard I liked to moonlight and spend my weekends fixing someone else's flub up (that someone else is usually the homeowner). Everyone's brother's mailman's neighbor's sister will likely call you because they "got your number" from so and so. This won't always ring true for every trade, but typical DIY tasks that homeowners initially think "are easy" often turn out to be too complex for every piece and part that is on the shelves of the home improvement stores.

When I first started in the trade as an apprentice, I felt honored that someone would put their trust in me to "get the job done, " whether it was complex or easy. It only took me a year or so of doing side-job plumbing tasks in people's homes before I realized how much I loathed doing my job in my free time. At that time, I didn't understand how to say no; more than that, I didn't want to disappoint people by not helping them. I did odd plumbing jobs for family and friends and friends of friends, and the biggest challenge I had throughout a few years of trying to be a nice guy? Asking for money. It is the worst thing about having a desired skill by others, even though they ask you to use your skills and fix or replace whatever they need fixing. Too many times, I waited until the job was done before discussing compensation for my skills, education, and knowledge to get their project done when I should have been upfront the minute I agreed to help out. That was ultimately the game changer for me in doing "moonlighting" work for people; I'm just not good at asking people to compensate me for what my time was worth.

Skilled trade folks have to learn to say "no" to many things. Side work, for one, unless you want to do it while you are single and build up the bank account, which is completely understandable. For a tradesperson with a family, the decision is yours whether to spend time away from home doing side jobs. Take it from a person like myself who is nearing the finish line in a matter of years, and in retrospect, side jobs are not worth the time away from the family. You may also have to juggle overtime on projects if it's a hurry-get-it-done project. The skilled trades always seem to be behind, and I've worked more Saturdays and overnights in my career than I could count. And was it worth it? I'm not really sure. There were nights I didn't get to say goodnight to my kids, which wasn't fair to them, and those were nights that would never come back.

Remember, work-life balance isn't constant; it changes over time. In our line of work, sometimes there's a surplus of tasks; other times, there's a scarcity. We have plenty of work during busy times and more free time during slower periods. This fluctuation makes it tough to maintain a perfect balance, but we can't disregard the balance – neglecting it may negatively affect our families.

The work-life balance discussion is age-old, but it remains very important as you progress through your career. Skilled trades careers can be as demanding as any other career, and you'll want to consider that. The work-life balance discussion has resurfaced since the COVID-19 pandemic, as many of the 40 million people who partook in "The Great Resignations" are now back at work, but not necessarily in their pre-COVID-19 field.

Those workers have reassessed their careers and commitment to their job duties versus their time spent at home, and time at home far outweighs any of the perks they may have had before the pandemic. *Why is this important?*

It's important to remember that most skilled trades jobs cannot be completed at home, remotely, or in any other convenient setting. Hands-on technical work requires you to be in-person and available. Undoubtedly, you'll have to manage a work life and a home life while in your career - and if a pandemic-style major life event happens again, you'll need to balance a dynamic that millions of people and millions of businesses worldwide were not prepared to juggle.

As we move on from this chapter, remember that you get out of your career what you put into it, and if your work-life balance is off balance, that will be a problem that can easily be fixed, but you'll have to be mindful of what that or those problem(s) are and work to change that dynamic.

In the next chapter, we will dive deeper into the two sides of skilled trades work, union employment versus non-union (private company) employment.

6

THE TWO SIDES OF SKILLED LABOR

The labor movement, a powerful force in US history, originated as a response to the adverse working conditions and exploitation faced by many during the Industrial Revolution. It gained momentum in the late 19th and early 20th centuries as workers organized to demand better wages, reasonable working hours, and safer workplaces. Over the decades, the labor movement matured and evolved, witnessing milestones such as the establishment of labor unions, the fight for collective bargaining rights, and the advocacy for social and economic reforms.

During its growth, the labor movement achieved significant victories, including implementing child labor laws, workplace safety regulations, and introducing minimum wage standards. These achievements brought about improved conditions for workers across various industries.

The labor movement has recently adapted to changing socioeconomic landscapes, embracing technology and diversifying its focus to address issues such as gender and racial equality, healthcare, and equivalent growth in the skilled trades. As a result, today's labor movement is multifaceted. It continues to advocate for workers' rights, social justice, and economic equity while utilizing a combination of traditional and modern tactics, including online advocacy, strategic campaigns, and grassroots mobilization.

As the labor movement has evolved, two distinct paths have emerged. Each path offers a unique way to address the needs and concerns of workers: Collective Bargaining and Non-Collective Bargaining.

Collective Bargaining. Collective bargaining is also known as organized labor. It involves the formation of employee unions or representatives who join forces to negotiate with employers on various aspects of work, from wages and benefits to working conditions and job security. This collaborative approach amplifies workers' voices as they collectively advocate for their rights and interests.

Non-Collective Bargaining. Non-collective bargaining, or unorganized labor, revolves around individual negotiations between employees and employers, where each person independently navigates their terms of employment without the formal structure of a union.

ORGANIZED LABOR

Organized labor refers to workers' collective efforts, often through labor unions or other worker associations, to advocate for better working conditions, fair wages, and improved rights within their workplaces and industries. This organized approach empowers workers to negotiate as a united front with employers and policymakers, aiming to create a more balanced and equitable work environment.

At its core, organized labor seeks to be the voice of individual workers, enabling them to address concerns that might be challenging to tackle on their own. By pooling resources, knowledge, and influence, organized labor can engage in negotiations, collective bargaining, and advocacy campaigns to secure tangible improvements in areas such as wages, benefits, job security, and workplace safety. By fostering a sense of solidarity and providing a platform for workers to voice their needs, organized labor collectively plays a pivotal role in shaping workplace policies, labor laws, and broader societal discussions related to labor rights and social justice.

Below are some of the reasons organized labor regularly reminds its workforce are positives for choosing organized labor.

Collective Bargaining. Negotiating as a unified group gives workers greater bargaining power to secure improved wages, benefits, and working conditions.

Higher Wages. Organized labor often leads to higher average wages and more equitable pay distribution.

Better Benefits. Workers in organized labor often have access to enhanced healthcare, retirement plans, and other valuable benefits.

Improved Working Conditions. Labor unions advocate for safer workplaces, reduced hours, and better treatment of employees.

Job Security. Organized labor can provide contractual protections against unjust terminations and layoffs.

Legal Support. Unions offer legal assistance and representation in labor disputes, ensuring fair treatment.

Career Advancement. Collective efforts may provide training, skill development, and opportunities for career growth.

Work-Life Balance. Labor unions advocate for reasonable work hours, breaks, and time off, promoting a healthier work-life balance.

Social Protections. Unions often campaign for policies like family leave and anti-discrimination measures.

Voice in Decision-Making. Workers have a say in workplace policies, fostering a more inclusive and democratic work environment.

Employee Support. Unions provide emotional and financial support during strikes, disputes, or conflicts.

Fair Treatment. Organized labor helps prevent unfair treatment, discrimination, and favoritism.

Skill Development. Labor unions may offer training programs to enhance workers' skills and employability.

Political Advocacy. Unions engage in political activism to support worker-friendly legislation and policies.

Solidarity. Workers in organized labor benefit from a sense of camaraderie, mutual support, and community.

It's important to note that although organized labor organizations advocate for the equitable distribution of benefits for the collective group of workers, the specific benefits can vary based on the nature of the labor union, industry, and regional labor laws.

UNORGANIZED LABOR

Unorganized labor, in contrast to organized labor, is often characterized by individual autonomy and freedom in negotiating terms of employment. Workers who engage in unorganized labor have the flexibility to directly communicate their preferences and concerns to employers without the intermediation of a formal labor union. This can lead to more personalized negotiations tailored to individual needs and circumstances. Unorganized labor arrangements can also provide a sense of self-reliance, as workers advocate for themselves without relying on external representation.

Furthermore, unorganized labor can promote a dynamic and diverse job market. Without the confines of standardized collective agreements, employers may be able to offer unique and innovative compensation packages and benefits to attract workers. In this environment, businesses can respond more swiftly to changes in market demands and individual worker preferences, fostering a more agile and responsive labor market. Additionally, unorganized labor can create an environment where workers can directly negotiate their terms of employment, potentially leading to a stronger sense of personal ownership and responsibility for their careers.

While unorganized labor offers certain benefits, it's important to acknowledge that individual bargaining power may be limited compared to the collective strength of organized labor. In organized settings, workers can pool their resources and influence to negotiate for improved wages, benefits, and working conditions on a broader scale. The balance between the benefits of individual autonomy and the collective power of organized labor remains a significant consideration in discussions about the overall labor relations landscape.

In contrast to organized labor employers providing the reasons why a skilled worker should consider the organized labor side; the unorganized labor movement and employers provide these reasons as benefits to choosing a non-collective bargaining career path.

Flexibility. Workers can negotiate and make decisions independently without adhering to collective bargaining agreements.

Personalized Agreements. Individuals can directly negotiate terms tailored to their needs and preferences.

Direct Communication. No intermediaries, allowing for direct communication and immediate action between workers and employers.

Speedy Decisions. Individual workers can quickly make decisions regarding work hours, tasks, and projects.

Innovation. Unrestricted by collective agreements, unorganized labor can experiment with innovative work arrangements and roles.

Skill Diversification. Workers can pursue a broader range of skills and experiences, potentially leading to diversified career paths.

Varied Compensation. Compensation structures can be customized based on individual performance, contributions, and results.

Work-Life Balance. Individuals can adapt schedules and work arrangements to achieve a personalized work-life balance.

Direct Recognition. Employers directly acknowledge and reward personal achievements and contributions.

Market-Based Competition. Employers may offer competitive compensation and benefits to attract and retain skilled workers.

Minimal Bureaucracy. Unorganized labor avoids the administrative complexities often associated with collective agreements.

No Union Dues. Workers are not obligated to pay union dues or fees.

Independent Entrepreneurship. Unorganized labor allows individuals to pursue freelance or entrepreneurial opportunities.

Direct Accountability. Workers have a clear line of accountability for their performance and outcomes.

Professional Growth. Individuals have the autonomy to take ownership of their professional development and career trajectory.

It's important to note that while unorganized labor offers certain benefits, it may also lack the collective strength, legal protections, and negotiation power that organized labor can provide. The choice between organized and unorganized labor depends on individual preferences, industry norms, and local labor conditions.

Although it really has no bearing on this book or this chapter, I've been on the organized labor side of the plumbing industry for my entire career. I've worked alongside many unorganized labor plumbers in my career, and I'm proud to say I've forged some career-long and life-long relationships with plumbers and additional trades workers on both sides of this discussion

It really comes down to what is a better fit for you. Working in a union environment or a non-union union environment has pros and cons across the board. Today, if someone asked me whether I would do it the same if I had to do it all over again, I couldn't define my answer as I see the plusses and minuses for organized and unorganized labor. My dad had a successful career in a union labor setting, and joining a union apprenticeship was my choice for how I received my education. I never felt the need to leave the organization that provided me with the technical education I needed to succeed in my career.

For my entire career, I've had the mindset that people get to choose what they want to do in their career and how they will get there. To me, a plumber is a plumber, just like a registered nurse is a registered nurse.

If you were a CAD designer and we were chatting about work, I certainly wouldn't look you up and down and sideways if you told me you were working for a private company in a non-union setting - because I really don't have the right to judge anyone for their choices of where and why they work there.

You will have every right to choose exactly the roads you want to travel if you choose to pursue a career in the skilled trades, and no one has the right to judge or admonish you if your work environment is on one side of a labor movement or another.

The bullet points of each side of skilled trades have been provided for you; the rest is up to you.

In the next chapter, we will look at some of the technological advancements in the skilled trades that have propelled these occupations throughout the years, and we will look at up-and-coming technologies that further solidify the need for modernization and continued interest in skilled trades positions.

7

TECHNOLOGY AND THE FUTURE OF SKILLED TRADES

For centuries, skilled trades have played a vital role in the global economy. However, recent technological advancements have brought about substantial changes in the execution of these professions.

Emerging technologies, ranging from automation to virtual reality training and 3D printing tools, are starting to reshape the landscape of the skilled trades industry. In the topics below, we will examine how new technology is revolutionizing skilled trade occupations and explore the potential advantages that may come from this transformative shift.

We will also analyze the impact of these technological developments on job security within the field. Lastly, we will consider future trends that could significantly influence this sector.

Let's dive right in by looking at recent technological advances and how they affect the hands-on working world.

THE EFFECTS OF NEW TECHNOLOGIES

The landscape of skilled trades is rapidly evolving with the integration of new technology. These innovative tools and advancements are reshaping skilled trades professionals' methods, resulting in streamlined processes, heightened safety standards, and enhanced efficiency.

For instance, augmented reality is finding its place in the construction sector, revolutionizing worksite instructions and elevating project accuracy to unprecedented levels. Simultaneously, machine learning is harnessed to optimize production line workflows, offering cost-effective solutions for businesses. Moreover, new technology facilitates seamless communication and collaboration among skilled tradespeople, even across great distances.

In essence, the influence of new technology is directly altering the work approach of skilled trades professionals, opening up new opportunities and showing improved outcomes throughout many industries.

Some recent technological advancements and how that tech affects certain skilled trades are detailed below.

Automation. Automation and new technology have greatly impacted the skilled trades industry. People did a lot of manual work in the past, but with the rise of automation, machines now do many tasks. This has created a need for new specialized skills, which can lead to more job security in the long run.

Additionally, automation and new technology have made it easier for more people to learn these skills, especially those who were not well-represented before, like women and minorities.

As automation continues to become a crucial part of skilled trades across the country, it's important to understand that it's not replacing human skills and creativity. Instead, it's working alongside them to improve the industry.

Virtual Reality. Virtual Reality (VR) is changing how people learn and prepare for careers in skilled trades, and if you're considering entering this field, it's important to understand how VR can benefit you.

In the US and Canada, VR is becoming a major tool for training apprentices in the construction, mining, and aviation/aerospace fields. Instead of jumping right into real-world situations, apprentices can use VR to practice in life-like 3D environments. This allows them to refine their skills and handle different scenarios safely before working in actual industrial settings.

What's amazing is that VR technology now lets students use virtual tools and equipment, giving them the feeling of actually being in the workplace. This means you can learn how to do real tasks without any real-world risks. It's like a powerful practice tool that's becoming essential for training in many skilled trades.

So, if you're thinking about a career in the skilled trades, know that VR is opening up exciting new ways to learn and prepare for the job, making it safer and more effective than ever before.

Three-Dimensional (3D) Printing. Three Dimensional (3D) Printing is causing a major transformation in the United States' skilled trades, and if you're thinking about a career in this field, it's important to understand how 3D printing can benefit you.

This technology offers a lot of promise. It can reduce costs, improve precision, and even let us create customized tools and parts. This is a big deal in industries like automotive, construction, and aerospace, where 3D printing has proven to be effective.

In the skilled trades, 3D printing could bring several advantages. It can speed up production, strengthen structures, and create more refined mechanisms. What's especially cool is that 3D printing allows us to make tools and parts in unique shapes and sizes that traditional manufacturing methods can't easily achieve.

If you're considering a career in the skilled trades, just know that 3D printing is entering many industries. It's not quite clear as of 2022 what role 3D printing will have in the hands-on skilled careers of the future. Although it brings many potential benefits to many industries, it could open up exciting opportunities for those seeking to join the skilled trades.

Artificial Intelligence (AI). The adoption of Artificial Intelligence (AI) is rapidly gaining momentum among US companies to enhance safety within their work environments.

AI exhibits the capacity to proactively identify and alert supervisors to potentially suspicious activities under challenging situations. Additionally, it can monitor employee adherence to safety protocols and regulatory measures. Furthermore, AI's analytical systems extend to evaluating safety vulnerabilities within specific workplaces, pinpointing areas of elevated risk, and recommending preemptive measures and protective gear for personnel.

Additionally, AI promises to eventually assume roles in hazardous tasks that would otherwise necessitate human exposure to danger. This technology provides an array of possibilities to elevate the safety standards for employees operating within a designated environment, thereby ensuring a safer work environment for all.

How New Technologies are Affecting Job Security in Skilled Trades. New technologies are having a positive impact on job security in skilled trades. As automation and artificial intelligence continue to advance, the demand for human workers to learn the systems required for those technologies in certain skilled trade industries is increasing.

For instance, welding robots are becoming increasingly common in shipbuilding, but those welding robots need human programming. In the past, this industry heavily relied on skilled human welders, but with the invention of welding robots, quality control is nearly impeccable by using welding robots that perform with precision. However, these robots need quality control measures in place, which means a new kind of welding work performed by humans at these shipyards.

While these technological advancements can enhance efficiency in some industries, they also create additional job requirements for humans in those fields. This means that individuals in these trades must actively acquire new skills and obtain additional certifications to aid in the efficiencies of these new technologies. Imagine becoming a hands-on, skilled shipyard welder whose main objective is to ensure the robot provides the precision welds required for that project.

Technological advancements like the welding robot are innovative and efficient, but robots are technology, and technology fails. There can never be an equal replacement for the human skilled worker.

As skilled trades continue to evolve, technology is making its way into the construction industry and all of the skilled trades in a big way. This change is happening faster than ever as we continue to face challenges like rising material costs, supply chain disruptions, and a global shortage of workers. A survey in 2018 showed that almost half of the personnel managers working in the field still rely on manual methods to collect essential data on job sites. This not only wastes time and resources but also slows down productivity. Many researchers have highlighted that construction productivity hasn't improved over the years due to disorganized processes, poor communication, and ineffective talent and project management. Technology has a significant role in shaping these trades' future.

The impact of the Coronavirus pandemic pushed the construction industry towards greater digitalization. As a result, a 2021 global capital projects outlook report by InEight revealed that 96 percent of contractors and project owners now believe in the potential of technology to boost productivity. Mobile apps simplify data collection for construction companies by consolidating information in one place, avoiding the challenges of retrieving data from various sources, which can lead to inaccuracies and complex data analysis. Artificial intelligence (AI) and machine learning technologies are highly regarded throughout the industry. This evolving attitude towards technology will shape the future of skilled trade work. Those who embrace these changes will gain a competitive edge, benefiting from data-driven decision-making, improved productivity, streamlined workflows, and stronger customer relationships.

Proven Technological Advancement

Imagine standing at the base of the Great Pyramid of Giza. This monument has stood for over 4,500 years, a testament to the incredible feats of construction by skilled stone masons in a civilization with basic tools carved out of stone, wood, and any other natural resource found throughout the desert 45 centuries ago. Built during the reign of Pharaoh Khufu in the 26th century BC, this architectural marvel stands as a remarkable example of human ingenuity, resourcefulness, and the power of skilled craftsmanship. Fast forward to the present day, where we find ourselves at the forefront of a new era in construction and skilled trades, one defined by technological advancements reshaping how we build, create, and innovate. Just as the construction of the Great Pyramid was an undeniable feat of its time, we are in the age of a transformation powered by cutting-edge tools, materials, and methods that promise to revolutionize the skilled trades industry.

Next, we look at a few industries that benefit from technological progress.

There are innovations across all industries served by skilled tradespeople, and the skilled tradespeople essentially had a hand in forming the ideas from which these innovations were created. Below are just a few across multiple industries.

Aerospace. Innovation: Advanced Composite Materials. Advanced composite materials, such as carbon fiber-reinforced polymers, have revolutionized aerospace manufacturing. These lightweight, strong, and corrosion-resistant materials enhance fuel efficiency and reduce emissions. Skilled trades workers in the aerospace industry are pivotal in crafting and assembling these complex composite structures.

Automotive. Innovation: Electric Vehicle (EV) Technology. The automotive industry is shifting significantly towards electric vehicles (EVs) and hybrid technology. Skilled tradespeople are essential for developing, assembling, and maintaining these vehicles. The transition to EVs promotes environmental sustainability and requires skilled workers to adapt to new technologies and systems unique to electric propulsion.

Construction. Innovation: Modular Construction. Modular construction involves building sections or modules of housing structures off-site in a controlled environment and assembling them on-site. This approach offers several advantages, including faster construction times, reduced waste, and improved quality control. Modular construction techniques transform how buildings are erected, leading to more efficient and sustainable projects.

Energy. Innovation: Smart Grid Technology. The energy industry is evolving with the implementation of smart grid technology, which uses advanced sensors, automation, and communication to optimize electricity distribution and consumption. Skilled tradespeople in the energy sector play a crucial role in installing, maintaining, and repairing the equipment and infrastructure necessary for innovative grid operations.

Manufacturing. Innovation: Additive Manufacturing (3D Printing). Additive manufacturing, commonly known as 3D printing, has revolutionized manufacturing processes by enabling the creation of complex components and parts layer by layer. This technology is increasingly used to produce prototypes, custom tools, and even end-use products, reducing waste, shortening production timelines, and allowing for greater design flexibility.

These innovations showcase how skilled trades labor is adapting to technological advancements, paving the way for more efficient and sustainable practices across diverse industries.

As we close out this chapter, I'll give you a short list of ten historical innovations in the construction industry that produced a positive return on investment within the industry it served.

Industrialization. Understanding the true impact of industrialization requires us to look further back than just the last few decades.

A groundbreaking innovation that greatly influenced our industry was the introduction of hydraulic and pneumatic devices in the mid to late 19th century. These advancements paved the way for developing earth-moving machinery and other equipment that has become integral to our infrastructure. These 19th-century technologies have played a pivotal role in significantly reducing the time and effort required for large-scale projects.

Advancing into the early 20th century, mechanization took on more advanced functionalities and capabilities. The 20th century marked the introduction of cherry pickers, concrete mixers, cranes, and power tools. During this period, the internal combustion engine emerged, proving to be a worthwhile replacement for traditional manual tools like hand shovels, wheelbarrows, and working animals. Instead, machinery like forklifts, tractors, backhoes, and bulldozers became the new norm.

Computer-Aided Design (CAD). During the pinnacle of the Middle Ages, ingenious architects, skilled drafters, expert stonemasons, and dedicated builders crafted some of history's most awe-inspiring structures using groundbreaking techniques for their era.

These methods persisted for centuries with very little alteration. However, in the latter half of the 20th century, a transformative technology emerged – computer-aided design (CAD) – forever altering the construction landscape.

Design clashes and conflicts became visible during the planning stages for the first time. Complex models of a building's mechanical systems could be seen on a screen that could provide a look at conflicts before they became a reality.

Previously, challenges like conflicting systems, electrical conduits, and HVAC ducting, which competed for the same physical space, perplexed architects and builders working with two-dimensional plans and section drawings. Adding CAD drawing to many construction projects can resolve these conflicts before a skilled trades worker moves onto the job site.

Mobile Devices. The impact of mobile technology on the construction industry is nothing short of transformative. Among the most significant improvements for contractors is the enhancement of project management. Utilizing smartphones and tablets, all trades providing labor on a project can collaborate seamlessly, sharing the same comprehensive information sources, regardless of location.

Real-time analytics have also been made possible in construction through mobile devices. Foremen can now monitor performance, conditions, and costs throughout the day using reporting tools, eliminating the need to compile reports at the end. Project managers leverage mobile business intelligence to foresee necessary adjustments, enabling immediate action to maintain schedules and budgets. Additionally, reporting apps allow for analytical insight for all parties, on-site or at the office. This integration of mobile devices has ushered in a new era of efficiency and connectivity within the construction industry.

Building Information Management (BIM). While CAD significantly reshaped the role of designers, Building Information Management (BIM) has emerged as an astonishingly versatile tool. It enables architects, engineers, contractors, and subcontractors to collaborate on intricate design and construction details using a shared database and computer model.

BIM involves all field personnel and office personnel in a project, working together on a comprehensive 3D model that encompasses every functional aspect of a structure. This comprises elements like pavements, beams, HVAC systems, electrical installations, plumbing, fire protection, and aesthetic features like walls, arches, roofs, and rails.

The collaborative nature of BIM spans the entire project timeline, allowing all parties involved to visualize and assess design decisions and to identify potential interferences and errors before any on-site work commences.

For contractors, this collaborative approach saves invaluable resources. Construction doesn't commence until every party has submitted their designs, ensuring that clashes are swiftly detected and resolved well before the construction phase begins.

As transformative as BIM is, it only marks the beginning of what's achievable. When paired with Connected Construction principles, the potential of BIM becomes even more attainable. Explore the culmination of these concepts in action in "The Great Library," a captivating docuseries that follows a global team as they reimagine a historic landmark using cutting-edge construction technology.

Prefabrication & The Evolution of Construction Industrialization. Constructing intricate and sizable components one piece at a time on-site, often exposed to the elements, presents its challenges. However, the emergence of off-site fabrication has brought remarkable efficiency.

For instance, consider a substantial heat exchanger expertly crafted in a vendor's workshop. Not only does it arrive at the site ready for integration, but it also benefits from superior parts and materials management and enhanced efficiency and productivity. This translates to higher returns on investment and reduced waste and inefficiency.

Substantial time savings in scheduling are achieved when elements like concrete insulated panels, timber frame panels, pump units, compressors, and instrument panels are meticulously fabricated in a controlled workshop environment instead of on-site. This results in components ready to be seamlessly interconnected once they arrive at the construction site.

The adoption of prefabrication and industrialized construction continues to grow within the industry. According to a SmartMarket report from Dodge Data & Analytics, 90% of contractors report experiencing improved productivity, enhanced quality, and increased schedule predictability compared to traditional construction methods. Furthermore, 61% of participants anticipate incorporating prefabrication techniques in at least 10% of their upcoming projects within the next three years, marking an increase from the current 44% utilizing this approach.

Robotic Total Stations (RTS). The conventional approach to laying out building services on a site involves a team using building drawings and a tape measure, level, and theodolite—an instrument for measuring angles. While effective, this method falls short when dealing with more intricate structures. It's time-consuming, prone to errors, and can result in clashes between various building services and prefabricated systems.

Robotic Total Stations (RTS) have emerged as a game-changer. An electronic theodolite combined with electronic distance measurement, RTS, can be operated remotely. A single individual can carry out the layout task by using a tablet with the appropriate software. RTS brings enhanced efficiency, accuracy, reduced errors, and less paperwork, ultimately decreasing labor costs. This innovative technology redefines building layouts, particularly for complex projects.

Digital Twins & Digital As-Builts. While the term "digital twins" was coined in 2002, the concept and application of digital twins and digital as-builts have been quietly shaping industries for decades. As far back as the 1960s, NASA used and promoted this technology. They employed a digital replica of Apollo 13 to engineer solutions and avert catastrophe.

The adoption of digital twins is rising within construction, steering project teams away from labor-intensive manual documentation. A digital twin or digital as-built stands as a virtual clone of a physical asset, furnishing real-time data throughout all construction and maintenance phases. These digital replicas predict carbon footprints, simulate scenarios, and glean real-time insights through embedded sensors.

Digital twins and as-builts are invaluable tools for skilled trade workers. Enabling swift decisions regarding operational and maintenance costs through design and construction information. In the field, these digital counterparts empower predictions about materials and labor.

Looking ahead towards the future, the potential for autonomous digital twins and as-builts is a reality. Envision a scenario where these entities learn and act independently on behalf of users. In the present, guided by Building Information Modeling (BIM), they are solidifying their role as pivotal players in the ongoing digital metamorphosis of the construction industry.

Sustainable Building Materials. The construction industry is steering towards sustainable building practices in the quest to slash carbon emissions. A pivotal aspect of this movement involves using sustainable building materials, ranging from Cross-Laminated Timber and reclaimed wood to bamboo, recycled rubber, and a myriad of groundbreaking alternatives. Picture a structure crafted from straw bales, rammed earth, Hempcrete (a hemp plant-derived concrete-like material), or frock (a steel dust-based concrete substitute). Remarkably, some of these materials reduce carbon emissions and absorb and sequester carbon dioxide, rendering them carbon-neutral.

Opting for sustainable building materials isn't solely an environmentally sound choice; it yields cost benefits, enhances structural energy efficiency, and enhances property value. With operational expenses reduced, overall construction costs can decrease by 5 to 15 percent, contingent on the specific eco friendly materials and methods used for production. Additionally, regulatory incentives in certain regions favor the appeal of sustainable construction.

The demand for sustainably-crafted buildings is soaring. Such structures often boast higher occupancy rates and rental fees than their conventional counterparts. Additionally, green building materials hold the potential to enhance occupant health. When embracing eco-conscious construction, it's a wise investment for the industry, occupants, and the planet at large.

Personal Protective Equipment (PPE). While Personal Protective Equipment (PPE) may not boast the same level of technological complexity as other entries, its impact on the construction industry's health and safety landscape over the past four decades is undeniable.

Take, for instance, the regulatory strides made in the UK to ensure employee well-being. Regulations mandating that employers provide suitable PPE to workers exposed to health and safety risks were established in 1992, falling under the Health and Safety at Work, etc. Act, which was enacted in 1974.

A performance assessment of this act in 2008 revealed a remarkable decline of 73 percent in fatal employee injuries and a 70 percent reduction in reported nonfatal injuries between 1974 and 2007 in the UK.

Across the Atlantic, the Occupational Safety and Health Act of 1970 ushered in OSHA in the United States. Other nations globally followed suit, implementing PPE regulations around the same period or shortly after.

Despite these regulations, a persistent need for safety remains on construction sites. While construction workers constitute only 6 percent of the U.S. labor force, they account for 20 percent of worker fatalities. This underscores the imperative for ongoing PPE innovation. Looking forward, PPE could encompass novel advancements such as exoskeletons and refined designs, further enhancing safety in the industry.

The (Digital) Cloud. Cloud computing is like the beating heart of changes happening in the construction industry. Before the cloud, we had limited space on our devices for project data. But now, we can use powerful machines in the cloud to access from anywhere. This means we have almost endless storage, and all our job sites can be connected.

The cool thing about cloud computing is that it gives everyone real-time access to data. This makes it super easy to share and work together. We don't have to waste time meeting in person to talk about progress or worry about running out of space on our devices.

Using the cloud to store project data makes a lot of sense for contractors. A survey by the Associated General Contractors of America and Sage Construction and Real Estate found that 85% of contractors already use or plan to use cloud solutions. Cloud computing makes storing and finding data simple, and it's a great way to keep data safe from loss, damage, or theft. It's like a protective shield for our data, making it easy for the whole team to access what they need.

Technology isn't going anywhere within the skilled trades - that is very apparent. Every year, there seem to be multitudes of new innovations that prove to strengthen the efficiency of working in a skilled trade. Whether it's new types of tools that prove to be more ergonomically correct or processes in which to produce, design, or build something or many things, new ways of arriving at the same result are gaining ground within the trades, and I'm all for it.

8

THE FORK IN YOUR ROAD

I have given you a massive amount of information in this book already, and I can assure you it all has been for the purpose leading up to this chapter.

As your high school days come to a close, you will reach a fork in the road. You, and you alone, will need to decide on the best path for your entry into the adult working world of your career. I'm not saying don't listen to suggestions made by your parents, school counselors, relatives, or peers; I'm simply stating that you get to make the right decision *for you*.

I've stated it multiple times in this book and I'll repeat it: *I am not anti-college.* I firmly believe that college is an excellent choice for certain types of students, but not every high school student is ready to go off to a four-year collegiate program a few months after their commencement from high school.

That is why I wrote this series of three books: to help students fully understand that no matter what anyone says -

it's entirely acceptable to have reservations at 18 or 19 years old about signing up for an education that may plausibly leave you with years of student loan repayments.

In certain professions, college is essential. Future doctors or lawyers, or those seeking a comprehensive education in the history of (just about anything), stand to benefit from a bachelor's degree initially and likely a master's program or more. Occupations that take years of specialized and targeted intellectual hands-off educations are worth the years spent in college if that makes the most sense.

I regularly give vocational career presentations to young adults and their parents, and a common misconception persists among many high school graduates or those contemplating an alternative to college – the notion that college or university is an obligatory path to career success.

It's worth saying that the college or university experience isn't a perfect fit for everyone. In 2021, a staggering 24% of first-year college students didn't finish their freshman year, resulting in a substantial number of individuals who, after enrolling full-time, realized that the college route wasn't for them. As the average first-year college debt hovers around $18,000, those 24% of first-year college students are now paying off student loans as you read this book.

An alternate career path is excellent for a young adult like yourself who may be inclined toward skilled, hands-on careers. Opting for an apprenticeship in the skilled trades instead of a traditional collegiate education can pave the way to a lifelong, sustainable, and lucrative career. The trades offer a trajectory toward a stable job or even future entrepreneurship. Apprenticeships, typically conducted in immersive, hands-on work environments, frequently provide a more streamlined learning process than traditional four-year degrees.

DECISIONS

Everything leading up to your senior year of high school has been to prepare you for commencement from your high school and your entry into the adult world. I'm guessing nowhere along the way did any administrators from any of your schools, or likely anyone else for that matter (save for your parents, maybe), sit down with you and have blatantly honest discussions with you about ALL of the options available when you walk out of your high school for the final time.

As we are nearing the end of this book, I want you to do just a quick check-in with yourself as you now assumedly have a fair bit more information about alternative options after high school than you had before reading this book or any of the three Career Planning For Teens books in this series.

The decision you have ahead of you about college, career, and post-secondary education is a difficult one; I completely understand that, and it's entirely normal for it to be complicated. I had no clue when I was your age what I wanted to do with my life, and if you've read the introduction to this book or read *Apprenticeship Career Planning For Teens,* you already know that I dropped out of high school. I've never regretted that decision, even today, some 30+ years after I did so. Our decisions follow us for life, and do you know what? *That isn't always a bad thing.*

In retrospect, my decision(s) to drop out of high school, then drop out of college, and follow that up by also dropping out of technical school were excellent

In 2005, at a commencement speech delivered to the graduating student body of Stanford University, Steve Jobs, the 1971 co-founder of Apple, stood at the podium in a cap and gown and said, *"It was impossible to connect the dots looking forward when I was in college. But it was very, very clear looking backward ten years later. You can't connect the dots looking forward; you can only connect them looking backward. So you must trust that the dots will somehow connect in your future".*

There aren't any dots to connect until we create the dots that we can look back on months or years later. My early dots led me to a lucrative and successful career in the skilled trades. Additional opportunities for career advancement, outreach to young adults, and educating apprentices in a vocational apprenticeship setting would lend themselves to being my connecting dots that Mr. Jobs spoke about in 2005.

Never for a minute in my career have I ever wished I'd gone a different path. The skilled trades have brought me more success than I ever imagined as a young man. I am very grateful for the hard work I've done, for the mentors I've had, and for the ability to connect with young adults who, although already have so much in their lives to be anxious about, are usually always willing to listen to my suggestions for them as they progress forward in their high school careers.

SIGNING DAY

As a high school student, you probably know what "signing day" is. In high schools all across the country, the elite athletes who have worked tirelessly to outperform each other, themselves and other students they've met on the playing field have a ceremony to "sign" and announce their choice for where they will attend college to play the sport they've been recruited to play at the collegiate institution.

As a high school student, signing day was not a thing many decades ago. I first learned about this signing day ceremony when my kids were at the high school level, and it still makes me roll my eyes just a bit. Public and private school systems want to create pomp and circumstance around a young man ot young lady signing paperwork that solidifies their intention to play their sport for a particular college or university. The athlete's family, friends, coaches, and mentors usually attend the signing day ceremony. The athlete signs a commitment letter of intent, puts on a jersey or a ball cap of their intended college or university, cameras flash, and maybe there's a quick interview by a local cable access channel, and then it's done.

High school signing days have become quite the phenomenon in the United States, and sometimes these signings are documented on National news channels if a particular high school athlete is expected to be the next best thing entering the collegiate sports market.

Career signing days are also a thing. I'm guessing you didn't know that a "career signing day" was happening nationwide in high schools. These career signing days seem to be not nearly as impressive as an athletic signing day for high schools, and these career signing days typically don't get media attention like athletic signing days do. In the US, during the 2021-2022 school year, 33 states participated in "career signing day." More and more states are recognizing career signing days as beneficial for students, businesses, apprenticeships, or jobs programs, partnering with career signing day high schools to recruit the next generations(s) of the workforce and ready young adults for transitions into the working world. These career signing days are one creative way that marketers in the hardest hit industries with labor shortages have come up with to generate interest in high school students entering a potential lifetime career skilled trade position immediately after high school.

In the United States, SkillsUSA is paving the way for private and public high schools nationwide to have their own career signing days to close the gap in the projected shortfall of skilled workers for the next three decades. SkillsUSA is a national organization that empowers students to develop and enhance their skills in various trade, technical, and skilled service professions. Through hands-on competitions, leadership development, and career-focused education, SkillsUSA provides students with opportunities to excel in construction, engineering, healthcare, culinary arts, and more. The organization promotes teamwork, professionalism, and a strong work ethic, preparing young individuals for successful careers and fostering a skilled workforce that meets the demands of various industries.

In my 25 years as a skilled tradesperson, I have seen a slight rise in the interest in skilled trades among high school students and also have seen interest in a four-year college plan begin to wane. The Coronavirus pandemic helped shed some light on the thought processes about the skyrocketing costs of college compared to the available alternatives, and as the pandemic receded and allowed the US to gain back some normalcy, the interest in a four-year college degree seems to have diminished ever so slightly. This indicates that the messages about multiple paths available for young adults are picking up speed.

As a high school student, you likely already have college or an alternative plan on your mind. You're nearly at the fork in the road that will set your adult working life in motion, and you'll need to weigh the pros and cons of each of your options and make the best decision you can make based on the information you have.

This book has never been to talk you out of a college path; its primary goal is to educate you on a specific alternative way to enter your adult working career that starts with minimal cost for education and provides years of healthy income.

CROSSROADS

As we near the end of the last chapter of this book and the end of this series of books to help young adults like yourself make fully educated decisions for your adult working world future, I would remind you that there is a decision ahead of you. Your parents, peers, school counselors, or others who might display a vested interest in your success and future well-being may influence this decision slightly.

I am certainly not going to tell you to drown out the conversations that these concerned folks might be having with you;

I'm just reminding you that it's entirely acceptable to listen to what others are saying or suggesting, take a mental note of their thoughts, and keep moving on in your decision-making process.

Ten or twenty years after your high school graduation, will all those people still be as interested in your future as they may be right now? *Probably not.* That's not to say they won't have care or concern for your general well-being; I'm only saying (as I'll put my parent hat back on here) that parents always wish their children the absolute best. That's a natural feeling for parents as we all want our children to be the most successful person ever walking the earth.

You are going to have to define what your success looks like. Unfortunately, you might need to start doing that before you graduate high school, as those visions of what your life will look like in your twenties, thirties, and forties aren't just a "dream sheet" - instead, they're mental goals that we all have daydreams about, and you will too.

With these three books in your career decision-making arsenal: *Financially Smart Career Planning For Teens (Sugardog Publishing, 2023), Apprenticeship Career Planning for Teens (SugarDog Publishing, 2023),* and *Skilled Trade Career Planning For Teens (SugarDog Publishing, 2023),* you will have nearly every bit of information at your fingertips to be thoroughly educated in the biggest workforce marketplace that (for the most part), does not require an expensive college degree to become successful and live a very comfortable life.

Are skilled trades sometimes hard work? ***Yes.***

Do the skilled trades mean that you'll be in a career that gets lots of social media attention? *Probably not.*

Are the skilled trades a path to a lucrative career often paying six figures? *Absolutely yes!*

You will need to use these three books as your Road Atlas for doing enough research to decide whether a traditional four-year college plan is the right choice for you or if you'd rather enter the workforce directly after high school. Heck, you could even take a gap year to get some traveling done or even decompress from your just completed thirteen years of school.

The point is that these three books provide nearly everything you'll need to make the right decision.

In Financially Smart Career Planning Teens, we dissected the cost comparison between traditional college costs and the lower-cost vocational option, which is a great way to get your education portion completed before entering the workforce. However, vocational or technical colleges have tuition, as you'll likely be in class daily (like in college). Still, you are on a single-track education path and being educated on specific career-needed education topics. If you enrolled in a vocational school in an electrician program, you'd have the whole education on everything you need to know to be successful as an electrician; you just wouldn't likely have the field-required hands-on experience yet.

If you went to technical school to become a draftsperson, you'd learn all there is to know about the software programs drafters use to provide the blueprints to the field workers who, in turn, will construct the building you just created a set of blueprints for. You likely wouldn't have the practical (real world) knowledge of how to draw some aspects of that building, though, without having some time walking through buildings to understand the "job conditions" that can affect how a set of blueprints gets produced.

Vocational or technical school is a valid way to enter the trades; it's just not the full scope of training you'd need to succeed right from day one. Vocational or technical schools offer grants and student loan programs. As the tuition is much lower than traditional college, student loans for hands-on career educational institutions are much easier to swallow. The cost of vocational-type schools averages about USD 20,000 for an entire two-year program, which is the typical timeframe for vocational programs.

In *Apprenticeship Career Planning For Teens*, you had the opportunity to learn about the lowest-cost way to enter into skilled trades, and that is through government-approved and sponsored apprenticeship programs across a wide array of industries in the US, UK, and Canada. Apprenticeships pay you to learn on the job from the experienced workers in the field you chose, and your schooling would typically happen once a week during the day or maybe a few evenings a week. Apprenticeships usually have their own training centers, so you'd be in a vocational school-like environment that closely resembles a college setting.

Apprenticeships may be a longer commitment than a vocational school, as apprenticeships differ in program lengths between industries. In the construction industry, the typical apprenticeship is between 3 and 5 years, while in some occupations in the medical industry, apprenticeships range between 1 and 3 years.

There are many options available for apprenticeships, and each industry that offers apprenticeships constantly needs a replacement workforce as the retirements happening in those industries far surpass the newly interested, younger generation of replacement workforce.

What does this mean for you? It means that an apprenticeship is nearly guaranteed if you're interested in an apprenticeship in any industries mentioned in Apprenticeship Career Planning For Teens and opportunities you discover through your additional research.

This book, *Skilled Trade Career Planning For Teens,* is the last piece of the puzzle on securing a lucrative career that will provide a lifetime of work, excellent pay and benefits, and a great retirement outlook. I believe I said it previously in this book; still, I'll repeat it - if working in the skilled trades (also known as blue-collar occupations) wasn't lucrative, didn't provide a solid financial future for its workers, and provided anything less than worthwhile retirement options, interest would have died off hundreds of years ago for skilled trade and skilled labor careers.

Occupations that require hands-on workers to get the job done have been getting the job done globally for hundreds or even thousands of years. Many years ago, the term "skilled trade" wasn't used. Still, this 21st-century world we live in was built by the hands of humans and will continue to be made, remodeled, demolished, and built again, all using skilled trades to perform every function of the building.

You are at a crossroads in life right now as you're in high school and have some decisions about what you want to do for the rest of your life. That is a tough decision for a young adult in high school, but it is the reality. Your school days will be over soon, and then you can enter the workforce or take another path like college that delays your ability to start your career debt-free.

By choosing a career in the skilled trades, you can be assured you'll have a lifetime of steady work, a healthy wage and benefit package, and a foundation for retirement that can easily be built on as your career progresses forward.

You've read this far in the book, so it must mean that you are still interested in learning more about the skilled trades and the lifestyle that can be had with a career in the trades. I hope you further investigate a skilled trade occupation that will suit you.

FINAL THOUGHTS

Well, my friends, we have come to the end of this book, and we have also come to the end of what I had never intended to be a three-book series on Career Planning For Teens (how much can one person go on and on about the subject after all?).

Immediately after I finished the first book, Financially Smart Career Planning For Teens (SugarDog Publishing, 2023), I realized another book was necessary as I barely scratched the surface of apprenticeships in that book.

I think it was only two days after Apprenticeship Career Planning For Teens (SugarDog Publishing, 2023) was published when I realized I had provided only two-thirds of the complete picture of how life and career in the trades bring the lucrative financial freedom that I think many people are looking and hoping for in a career; and that's what led me to write this final book. I hadn't provided the complete picture, which would have left you in the dark on the final piece of the career decision you likely started reading this series for.

I know I've given you loads of information in this book, which was my intention. I needed to provide you with as much information as possible to give you the upper hand on your decision-making capability for your career and your post-secondary education choices.

EMPTY DEGREES

In the early 1990s and 2000s, most high school graduates entered college into business education. Business was the hot marketplace for a decade or so back then, and there were so many business degrees being offered by colleges it almost seemed like colleges were randomly creating these degrees to feed the wanton desire for high school students to say they're getting a business degree. In my opinion, the late '90s and early 2000s were the years when collegiate institutions systematically tipped the scales on affordable college degrees, which were no longer a reality during those years.

Colleges offered business degrees such as Bachelor of Business Administration, Bachelor of Commerce, Bachelor of Economics, Bachelor of Finance, Bachelor of Marketing, and so on. There were so many business bachelor degrees available I think colleges just randomly inserted some business-related words behind "Bachelor of." Aside from the bachelor's degrees I just listed, there were random business bachelor's degrees in management, international business, entrepreneurship, accounting, human resource management, information systems, and more.

Technology and business were booming during those years, and the colleges of the United States didn't want to be left out of the money grab from the millions of high school seniors who graduate every year.

During those years, Wall Street was experiencing a tremendous boom. New technology known as the internet was rapidly gaining ground, and seemingly, the ultimate career success involved occupying an office space with a computer, raking in small fortunes if you had a Bachelor of (business something). These career paths were readily available and plentiful during those times. Today's young adults like yourself have similar dreams of stable and lucrative employment; however, the path toward making a small fortune right out of college is less attainable.

Although the job market is constantly changing, for hundreds and hundreds of years, there have always been skilled workers to do the jobs that, although they might not seem glamorous, are lucrative and constant. The current job marketplace in the 2020s is begging young adults like you to broaden your horizons beyond conventional white-collar careers to pursue stable and lucrative vocations.

Aside from my deep-rooted mindset that every high school student needs to have the entire spectrum of information presented to them regarding career choices after high school, I am compelled every day to help young adults understand that blue-collar jobs are no less important than those people who create new technologies that set the US apart from the rest of the world.

My goal with these books has been to help you understand that blue-collar skilled trades occupations are something that young adults like yourself should be proud to say they are interested in pursuing. Skilled tradespeople have built every country on this planet going as far back as history books tell us. Although the skilled trades have always been stereotyped as being a career for people who couldn't make it in college or people who maybe were "rough around the edges," the skilled trades have provided Americans with great jobs for centuries.

Throughout every chapter in this book, I've told you why you should consider the trades a viable option for a lifelong, sustainable career. I will reiterate a few of those points and provide five reasons in which you could argue your point of choosing the trades over a career where you'll need a bachelor's or something similar to gain an entry-level job with entry-level pay.

Apprenticeship and Trade Schools are far less expensive than college. Careers in skilled trades offer many great benefits, with education being pivotal. While the value of a four-year bachelor's degree needed for specific industries is undeniable, it comes with certain drawbacks, especially concerning the constantly rising cost. Recent data reveals that college tuition expenses have surged by over 200% since 2000, outpacing inflation and wage growth. The financial strain becomes evident when tuition rises at an average annual rate of around 5%, compared to an inflation rate of about 2-3%. This is further compounded by the fact that student loan debt in the United States has reached a staggering $1.7 trillion as of 2023, impacting millions of graduates.

To put it into perspective, many students graduate burdened by substantial debt. Roughly 44.5 million Americans hold student loan debt, with an average debt per borrower surpassing $38,000. Additionally, around 60% of college graduates are estimated to carry some debt upon completing their degrees. The financial obligations resulting from student loans can linger for years, affecting major life decisions such as homeownership, marriage, and starting a family.

In contrast, vocational training programs for skilled trades typically span six months to two years and cost considerably less. Recent figures suggest that the average cost of trade school and vocational programs hovers around $10,000 to $25,000 for a two-year hands-on program. Even if financed through loans, the total debt accrued is notably lower than a traditional four-year degree.

This reveals a noticeable gap in opportunity costs between the two paths. While college students spend several additional years in school, incurring substantial costs, those pursuing skilled trades often enter the workforce sooner, with significantly lower debt ahead of them, if any debt at all. The practical experience gained during trade education careers readies individuals for immediate employment in various well-paying industries and professions.

Additionally, it's essential to acknowledge that not all high school graduates are equipped for a college environment. The transition from home life to college independence can be daunting, and statistics indicate that college dropout rates are rising. Roughly 30% of students enrolled in bachelor's degree programs drop out before completing their education, facing financial setbacks and the lack of a degree.

Trade schools provide a more gradual transition to the adult working world. They offer targeted training, often closer to home, with a hands-on approach that suits certain learning styles better. These programs prepare individuals to enter the workforce, accruing valuable skills and earning potential without the daunting financial and time commitments associated with traditional four-year degrees.

While the advantages of a four-year college degree are undeniable for some people, the shifting economic landscape indicates that exploring skilled trades as an alternative is necessary. As tuition costs rise and student loan debt grows, trade schools offer a realistic and cost-effective pathway to meaningful employment and financial stability.

Skilled trade occupations pay very well. Even if you're worried about how much college costs, many still believe that the investment is worth it because it can boost how much money you earn throughout your life.

The concern about how much money you'll make working in the skilled trades is a big reason why young adults like you might not consider working in the trades. While money isn't the only important thing to consider when choosing a career, it does matter. Many think that jobs in offices pay more than jobs that involve physical work. And if we're talking about the people who earn millions yearly, most are not tradespeople—they've usually gone to college. But those super-rich folks make up only a tiny part of all the people who work.

If we look at the average earnings—what most of us can expect to earn in our jobs—tradespeople earn about the same or even more than people in other careers. A study in Michigan found this to be true. The top earnings might be higher in office jobs, but the typical payments are better for tradespeople. For trades, the hourly pay ranges from $25 to $55, with most trades being right around $48 or so on the paycheck, plus a benefits package. The benefits package(s) available to trades workers also comes with a value; it just can't be recognized as income. However, "fringe benefits," as discussed earlier in this book, happen in the background and wouldn't go into your pocket as a cash payment. I've known skilled trades workers whose benefits packages were worth $26 an hour, and I've also known folks whose benefits packages were worth up to $39 an hour. Remember, those benefits packages cover your healthcare, pension contributions, and maybe an annuity (a cash account supplement to a pension, usually with ties to the stock market). A vacation pay account might be a fringe benefit, in addition to tuition assistance (for the worker's spouse or children) or any host of additional "perks" that make up the skilled trade workers' pay.

With all of that being said, if you were to take some average hourly pay rates and fringe benefit packages and add them together to come up with an "on paper" hourly rate, you will see that there are skilled trades in specific industries that are making significantly, perfect money. I used the term "on paper" as that's what it's called when you get hourly monetary compensation and fringe benefits. Fringe benefits typically are not taxed, as those benefits are not directly deposited to you, the worker - rather, they are benefits that, although they do have a value per hour that you work, don't come to you in the form of monetary income. Fringe bene-fits don't add to your yearly gross or take home pay, but they are valuable and shouldn't be considered anything else than something of value that happens in the background when you are working.

Here's an example: Let's say Sarah is an emergency room nurse. Sarah makes $ 39.75 per hour at her nursing job. If we multiply Sarah's hourly wage by 2040 hours in a working year (40 hours each week multiplied by 52 weeks), her before-tax income would be $ 82,680 yearly. Sarah has a fringe benefits package that provides her and her family with medical insurance, and for each hour she works, her employer contributes $ 8.50 to her healthcare cost. Sarah's employer also contributes $ 4.40 per hour to a retirement pension plan and another $ 2.25 per hour to an annuity supplementing her pension.

Sarah's "total package" pay structure would be her taxable hourly base pay of $ 39.75 per hour plus her non-taxable employer contributions each hour Sarah works; healthcare at $ 8.50, a pension contribution of $ 4.40, and a supple-mental pension (annuity) of $ 2.25 each hour. The "fringe benefit" package Sarah makes per hour is valued at $ 15.15 per hour that Sarah works. If we add Sarah's taxable hourly pay of $ 39.75 to her non-taxable fringe benefit pay of $ 15.15 per hour, Sarah is making a "total package" hourly pay of $ 54.90 an hour, which is $ 114,192 each year - but only the hourly pay is taxable, not the fringe benefits. Sarah is making $ 114,192 yearly "on paper."

Nurse Sarah's example pay structure is very typical in the skilled trades, and remember - we looked at Sarah, a nurse. Over a hundred more occupations with trades pay are structured just like that, and many pay much more than Sarah's occupation. Sarah's example showed us that a skilled trade occupation can get close to the six-figure a-year range and that the six-figure term is related only to a person's taxable income. Depending on the region of the United States where you live and work, multitudes of skilled trades earn six figures each year from their taxable hourly pay. Typically, the six-figure occupations are found more in the construction industries, but that's not to say that tech or healthcare industries aren't nearly there.

All skilled trades pay well; many are structured like Nurse Sarah's example. I'll summarize this point of the very good and lucrative pay structure within most skilled trades like this: knowledge is power, and knowledge has a lot of value. What blue-collar, hands-on, skilled trade workers do daily has value, yet not everyone wants to do those occupations. If everyone wanted to do what we do, there wouldn't be a multi-industry labor shortage. I wouldn't be writing these books trying to enlighten you about the fact that you can enter into a very well-paying career without spending a dime on a traditional four-year college that provides a piece of paper (called a degree) at the end of the four years that validate you've paid an excessive amount of money for an education that millions of your peers also received. Now, you will fight with those peers to land a job and earn a bare minimum salary. Additionally, just a few months after receiving that piece of paper the college sent you, you'll also be spending hundreds of dollars a month as you now have to start paying the student loan lending company what you owe them for funding your degree.

An imbalance in the supply and demand. You can follow my analogy if you know just a little about supply and demand. Imagine that business and the skilled trade workforce operate under the terms of supply and demand (actually, they work that way). When companies have a massive demand for skilled workers, they realize they need to "make it worthwhile" for the supply of workers to work for that business. That's when a company realizes it needs to pay the workers more than before to keep operating and profit from those skilled workers' labor.

When the supply of skilled workers is overflowing, business (the demand) understands that although they might not need more skilled workers, it might be nice to have a few extra hands to get the job done; so that business will take on those workers. Still, the amount those workers will be paid will decrease because so many people are available.

From the late 1990s until now (2023), there has been a grave imbalance in the supply and demand for skilled workers. Industries such as energy, manufacturing, construction, and technology have been seeing record profits after rising from the recession in the late 2000s. Yet, they cannot capture all available revenue streams as they don't have the workforce to provide the products that make their money.

There is a very recognizable skills gap in the United States, which is the driving factor within the imbalance. There are far more skilled trade jobs available than there are willing and able workers to take those jobs. The median wage for skilled trades in many industries has been trending upward for the last decade. The demand for workers is high, and the supply is low. Thus, the demand side (businesses) is willing to entice the supply side (skilled workers) with better wages, additional benefits, and a seemingly unending amount of work to be done.

When doing a bit of research on the skills gap for this book, I learned that among all careers in the US as of 2023, workers aged 25-44 make up nearly 48% of the entire workforce, and within the skilled trades, that same age group makes up 46% of those trades. People aged 45-54 make up 23% of the general workforce, but in the skilled trades, that age bracket makes up 33% of every skilled trade among the industries. This means there will be a skills gap for the foreseeable future, and the hands-on skilled trade jobs are not going away anytime soon.

The imbalance in the supply and demand for hands-on, technically educated workers has been apparent for decades; it's just not talked about very much in high schools. That's why closing the gap on that imbalance is not happening very fast - which is good for you as a young adult. It pretty much means you can have the "pick of the litter" for a skilled trade. The jobs are there; you just need to find one you'd like to do for the lifetime of your career.

I feel that as I say things like, "You just need to find one you'd like to do for the lifetime of your career," you, as a young adult, are having a hard time envisioning working in a career field for the next 30-40 years. I do not intend to bring you down or give you cause for stress about something that you may view as simple-minded. It's just the reality now that you are approaching your last days of high school. Unless you have the business acumen to be the next social media influencer with 62 billion followers, you will likely be in a singular field for your occupation. That singular field is likely where you'll experience all that life offers - like marriage, kids, your first house, vacations, home repairs, and more. That is the stark reality of the adult working world - you come out of high school into the adult world, and then it's time to become a productive citizen of society.

As I've said in the first two books in this series, I'll repeat it again for you: *working in the skilled trades is not glamorous*. No private jets in the trades are waiting to whisk you nationwide for a business meeting. There are no business conferences on tropical islands for a week. There are no conferences to attend in a foreign country, and no bonuses are given for hitting a million dollars in sales in a year.

The skilled trades occupations are day-in and day-out work. Working in the skilled trades is not monotonous; it has never been for me. Every day I go to work, I do the best job possible to earn my wage and get paid for my work every week. Do I care that I don't get recognition for my day-in and day-out work? No.

Do I wish I had taken a different path in life and maybe would have had the opportunity to spend every day in a business setting? **Absolutely Not.**

> **Job satisfaction.** In 2015, a study on job satisfaction was done on some of the largest corporations in America. One of the questions in that job satisfaction study was, "Would you prefer to have job security at work or to be able to use

your skills and abilities?". The results returned for that question alone tell a story of the shift in the paradigm about how workers value their occupations. Over 70% of respondents noted they'd feel more satisfied at work using their skills and abilities than having a secure position within a company that might not be challenging for them.

Indeed, everyone has days at work when the workload might be light, and they feel bored or disengaged, right? It's natural that is going to happen. Boredom, or disengagement at work, is a rarity for a skilled trade worker. People who work with their hands for most of their career experience a different kind of job satisfaction than people who don't work with their hands. The mental stimulation from using your hands to craft something tangible has proven to be a defining factor in why people in the skilled trades stay in their careers for their lifetime. Using specific knowledge to create something tangible and specific is rewarding.

Another important factor is the satisfaction you get from doing things you can physically see and touch, like fixing objects or building something, where you can see the actual results of your work. This can be more personally rewarding than spending 8 hours working on a computer spreadsheet. An author named Matthew Crawford talked about this in an article in the New York Times. He said that many of us do work that feels less real and more like a dream. When you work in an office, it's often hard to see what you've achieved by the end of the day. When the connection between what you do and the outcomes is unclear, and the responsibility is spread out, it's tough to feel like you're making a difference. Interestingly, about 40% of jobs in today's economy involve coordinating and mediating instead of directly creating or doing things.

Other important things to consider are having control over your work and balancing work and personal life. Nowadays, many people can access their work through the internet and smartphones, making it tough to disconnect from work. You might see work-related emails at night and respond without thinking. You might plan to spend a moment on the computer, but then it turns into a couple of hours because work is right there and seems urgent. This can make you feel tied to your email and your bosses, even if that was not intended. When you work with your hands, you have the advantage of being able to come home and leave your work behind. You're not always "plugged in," which gives you a better chance to relax your body and mind for the next day's work. Of course, you can work extra hours if you want to – plus, you can charge your customers more for your after-hours services if you do.

The skilled trades are immune to outsourcing. What you get paid is important, but it's the third most important thing in the study regarding how happy you are with your job. The most important thing is having a chance to use the skills you're good at, and the second most important thing is knowing your job is secure. So even if jobs in skilled trades might pay similarly to office jobs, for some people, these other things make skilled trades more appealing than sitting in a small office space.

In today's new way of doing business, there's no such thing as a completely secure job. Anything could happen to any company, and you might lose your job. However, some positions are more stable than others. Information technology and tech jobs are at risk of being taken over by robots or moving to other countries. But even careers that used to be very secure, like medicine and law, have started to be outsourced elsewhere.

In contrast, trade jobs can't be sent away to other places. While the need for bloggers might change, there will always be a demand for skilled workers like mechanics, electricians, plumbers, and welders. When you're locked out of your house, you won't be talking to robots on the phone; you'll call a locksmith to help you out. The roads and bridges we use daily are maintained by skilled trades workers in our own country. Big construction projects like skyscrapers won't be made in one place and then shipped over – remember, that only happened once with the Statue of Liberty. Unlike jobs in customer service, which can easily be moved elsewhere, careers that involve hands-on work can't be moved around that easily, if even at all.

A longtime advocate for skilled trades in the United States, Mike Rowe emphasizes an essential point in his book, "Profoundly Disconnected." He talks about how many of us are disconnected from the things that make our lives and society work smoothly every day (that's why the book has that title). Without people in the trades, our community would quite literally fall apart. Roads and bridges would crumble. Cars would break down and never get fixed; we wouldn't even have new vehicles to replace them. The power grid would fail, and we'd lose electricity. Plumbing would fail or get blocked, and we'd end up dealing with serious sanitation problems. It might not sound nice, but this is a reality we're facing. Our infrastructure is deteriorating right in front of us. The American Society of Civil Engineers gives our infrastructure a very low grade of D+. Recently, on a TV show called "60 Minutes," they discussed how our infrastructure is falling apart. This is a critical issue. Things will only worsen if we don't have more skilled tradespeople.

The five points I made above are the biggest takeaways from this book that you should make a mental note of, and remember these five points as your most vital talking points when your peers, parents, or any other person might be questioning why you're considering an occupation in the trades. As I've told you multiple times in this book and my two previous Career Planning for Teens books, the skilled trades aren't glamorous - *What they are is prosperous.*

The many industries begging for a replacement workforce are expected to beg louder and longer in the next decade. There are projected to be 15-18% more retirees in the skilled trade industries in the next two decades (2023 - 2043) than there were from the start of the 2000s until 2022. That means people like you can nearly "walk on" to a skilled trade career. Skilled trades careers always start with either an apprenticeship or a vocational school of some sort - and you absolutely could graduate high school one day and start your career in the trades the next day.

Besides the fulfilling work that comes with a skilled trade career, the fringe benefits and retirement benefits are nearly unmatched. I have twenty-six years into this career that I didn't know I'd be good at when I obliged my dad and signed up for an apprenticeship. I can't imagine having done anything else that would provide me with the same satisfaction, career advancement opportunities, and financial freedom as I've experienced from a hands-on skilled trades career as a plumber.

The very last thing I will leave you with in this book is a bit of wisdom from this half-century-old plumber that incessantly pushed himself to achieve things he never knew were possible for a high school dropout and two-time collegiate dropout.

I created a successful career in the skilled trades from virtually a pile of nothing. When I started my apprenticeship (as my dad had told me I needed to do), I never wanted to be a plumber and decided to do it for a while just for a steady paycheck. I was a mid-20s young man then, and a labor job didn't scare me as long as I was getting paid.

The only requirement of me when I started my apprenticeship was to show up on time, show up every day, and do exactly as I was told. None of the three requirements seemed like they were too hard to follow, so I did my part and worked Monday through Friday as they said I would be doing.

I started my first year of apprenticeship school not knowing much of anything related to plumbing as for the previous three or four months that I worked "in the trade," I was pretty much a trench digger that the experienced tradespeople would install their pipes in the trench I just labored over for hours. Then they would tell me to bury the pipes. I often thought, "So, you're telling me to dig a trench multiple feet deep and very long and then turn right around and throw all the dirt back in?".

After three or four of these exact scenarios, I realized I probably didn't want to do this for the rest of my working life, so I spent the next few months devising a plan on what next adventure in my life would pay me as much as I was earning as a first-year apprentice. My brain returned nothing in the form of results for that plan, so I shifted my mindset to thoughts like, "Well, I'm the highest-paid trench digger on this job," or something like, "If they're going to pay me this much money to dig their trenches, I better make these trenches the nicest ones they'll ever see."

Many years later, when I connected my dots looking backward, as Mr. Steve Jobs explained before his unfortunate passing, those dots told me that at the time I was digging trenches, I was already becoming self-aware about my career aspirations. I didn't want to dig trenches for my entire career, yet I made dang sure the trenches I dug were the ones that were talked about among the experienced workers.

I continued to do as I was told for a few more years as an apprentice, and then I woke up one day long after I had been reassigned to a different work detail and no longer a trench digger, and I realized that digging those trenches wasn't so bad.

That's kind of how things go as a skilled tradesperson. One day, you might be doing a task that you don't enjoy, but you're earning very good money for doing that task, so is it really that hard to perform it until the end of the work day? *No.*

We make our own way and pave our own path in our careers in the skilled trades. We create opportunities for ourselves where we can, and we take the opportunities offered to us if they fit into our career goals.

A career in the skilled trades offers a lifetime of steady work, excellent pay, great working benefits and retirement benefits, and the satisfaction of seeing the fruits of your education, skills, and labor at the end of the day.

Take it from me: There is zero downside to a career in the skilled trades.

I wish you all the best in your continued research and decision-making, and I know it's not easy as a young adult to think decades ahead of the moment you currently are in. Major life decisions are never easy, and even at my age, life decisions don't get any easier, that's for certain.

Trust your gut, as you're the only one you'll have to answer to in future decades about where your career has taken you, and how successful you feel your career has been.

With humble gratitude,

P.D. Mason

Spread the Word!

There's an exciting road ahead of you, and you're just at the start of it. This is your chance to help someone else discover their journey as a skilled tradesperson.

Simply by sharing your honest opinion of this book and a little about what you found here, you'll help other young people find the essential guidance they'll never get in high school.

Thank you so much for your support. Your role is vital, and I appreciate you tremendously.

Scan the QR code to leave your review on Amazon.

ABOUT THE AUTHOR

Paul Mason lives in the upper Midwest region of the United States with his wife and his trusted writing companion, a knee-high pit bull terrier mix named Sugar. Paul is an independent author writing for SugarDog Publishing and has written multiple fiction and non-fiction books on various topics and fictional storylines that resonate with his readers.

ALSO BY P.D. MASON

Financially Smart Career Planning For Teens: The Roadmap to Making Informed Decisions In An Uncertain Job Market, Prevent Feeling Overwhelmed & Analysis Paralysis To Achieve Affordable College Degrees(2023, SugarDog Publishing)

Apprenticeship Career Planning for Teens: A Comprehensive Guide to Securing Apprenticeships in High Demand Industries Without Taking on Years of College Debt (2023, SugarDog Publishing)

Travel Japan: Unveiling Culture, Language & Local Gems (2023, SugarDog Publishing)

8 Simple Techniques For Easy Kitchen Knife Sharpening: Keep Your Home Kitchen Knives Sharp Using Trusted Tools, Methods & Techniques Taught By Professionals! (2023, SugarDog Publishing)

REFERENCES

"5 Reasons a Skilled Trade Job Should Be Your next Career Move." *SharkBite*, 24 Sept. 2021, www.sharkbite.com/us/en/resources/blog/5-reasons-a-skilled-trade-job-should-be-your-next-career-move. Accessed 12 May 2023.

"5 Ways Tech Innovation Has Changed Skilled Trade Jobs." *ServiceTitan*, www.servicetitan.com/blog/5-ways-tech-innovation-has-changed-skilled-trade-jobs. Accessed 5 Sept. 2023.

"6 Safety Guidelines for Trade Workers." *Advantage Outfitters*, www.commercialvanshelving.com/blog/safety-guidelines-for-trade-workers/. Accessed 5 Sept. 2023.

"72 Trades to Learn for a Successful Trade Career." *Indeed Career Guide*, 23 June 2023, www.indeed.com/career-advice/career-development/learn-trades.

"90 Trade School Scholarships to Apply for in September 2023." *Bold.org*, 6 Sept. 2023, bold.org/scholarships/by-major/trade-school-scholarships/. Accessed 5 Sept. 2023.

Admin, N. T. I. "Do Trade Workers like Their Jobs? The Answer Is Yes!" *Northeast Technical Institute*, 24 Sept. 2021, ntinow.edu/do-trade-workers-like-their-jobs-the-answer-is-yes/.

Almond, Rob. "Council Post: How to Advance the Skilled Trades through Technology." *Forbes*, 5 Sept. 2022, www.forbes.com/sites/forbesbusinesscouncil/2022/05/25/how-to-advance-the-skilled-trades-through-technology/?sh=740b47f47b66. Accessed 5 Sept. 2023.

Bleich, Corey. "Hard Skills vs. Soft Skills: Examples and Definitions." *EdgePoint Learning*, 25 Mar. 2020, www.edgepointlearning.com/blog/hard-skills-vs-soft-skills/.

BridgeWorks. "Trades Myths Debunked: Women & Soft Skills." *Bridgeworks*, www.generations.com/insights/trades-myths-debunked-women-soft-skills. Accessed 5 Sept. 2023.

Buel, Zander. "Why There's a Higher Demand for Tradespeople Post-Pandemic." *Refrigeration School, Inc. (RSI)*, 8 Oct. 2021, www.rsi.edu/blog/skilled-trades/why-theres-a-higher-demand-for-tradespeople-post-pandemic/. Accessed 5 Sept. 2023.

Burkes, Lester. "Can Automation Replace Skilled Trades Workers?" *Learn a Skilled Trade*, 8 Apr. 2023, learnskilledtrades.com/will-skilled-trades-be-automated/. Accessed 5 Sept. 2023.

Chris. "4 Reasons Why You Should Consider a Skilled Trades Career." *MB HAYNES Corporation, Asheville NC*, 1 June 2022, www.mbhaynes.com/general-construction-blog-tips/why-consider-skilled-trades-career/. Accessed 5 Sept. 2023.

Cliffs, College. "21 In-Demand High Paying Technical and Trade Careers." *College Cliffs*, 30 Sept. 2018, collegecliffs.com/top-paying-in-demand-technical-trades/.

Crawford, Matthew. "The Case for Working with Your Hands." *The New York Times*, 21 May 2009, www.nytimes.com/2009/05/24/magazine/24labor-t.html.

"Debunking the Biggest Myths about Skilled Trades." *Vibration Analysis*, 1 June 2020, ivctechnologies.com/2020/06/01/debunking-the-biggest-myths-about-the-skilled-trades/.

Decker, Stanley Black &. "Drilling into the Skilled Trades Shortage: Stanley Black & Decker's Inaugural Makers Index Reveals Few Students Likely to Consider a Career in the Trades; Outdated Perceptions Key Drivers." *Www.prnewswire.com*, 5 Apr. 2022.

"Dispelling Myths about Women in the Trades | Pennco Tech." *Www.penncotech.edu*, 2 Dec. 2020, www.penncotech.edu/dispelling-myths-about-women-in-the-trades/. Accessed 5 Sept. 2023.

"7 Ways to Promote Work-Life Balance for Skilled Tradesmen." *PeopleReady Skilled Trades*, 30 Nov. 2021, skilled.peopleready.com/7-ways-to-promote-work-life-balance-for-skilled-tradesmen-tradeswomen/. Accessed 5 Sept. 2023.

Dunn, Erin. "24 of the Highest-Paying Trade Jobs in 2023." *Intuit Credit Karma*, 4 May 2023, www.creditkarma.com/income/i/highest-paying-trade-jobs#:~:text=Many%20trades%20can%20offer%20high. Accessed 5 Sept. 2023.

Farrington, Robert. "Trade Schools vs. Traditional College: What You Should Know." *Forbes*, 21 Feb. 2022, www.forbes.com/sites/robertfarrington/2022/02/21/trade-schools-vs-traditional-college-what-you-should-know/?sh=79eacd387638. Accessed 5 Sept. 2023.

"Five Technology Trends That Will Change the Skilled Trades." *Kitchen & Bath Business*, 6 Dec. 2021, www.kbbonline.com/news/blog/five-technology-trends-that-will-change-the-skilled-trades/. Accessed 5 Sept. 2023.

Freese, Derek. "Why a Job in the Skilled Trades May Be Right for You ": *Award Staffing*, 19 Mar. 2020, www.awardstaffing.com/why-a-job-in-the-skilled-trades-may-be-right-for-you/. Accessed 5 Sept. 2023.

Gustafson, Katie . "Yes, Trade School Scholarships Exist! Here's How to Get Them." *SkillPointe*, skillpointe.com/news-and-advice/yes-trade-school-scholarships-exist-heres-how-get-them.

HARVEY, DON . "How to Become a Master of Your Craft | Kforce." *Www.kforce.com*, www.kforce.com/articles/how-to-become-a-master-of-your-craft. Accessed 5 Sept. 2023.

"How to Choose the Right Skilled Trade for You." *NDC Trades*, 29 May 2023, www.ndctrades.ca/post/how-to-choose-the-right-skilled-trade-for-you. Accessed 5 Sept. 2023.

"Licensing Requirements for the Trades in the US [2021]." *Paschal Air, Plumbing & Electric*, 16 July 2021, gopaschal.com/licensing-requirements-for-the-trades-in-the-us-2021/. Accessed 11 May 2022.

Hudgeons, Victoria . "Your Guide to Trade Schools | BestColleges." *Www.bestcolleges.com*, 16 July 2022, www.bestcolleges.com/trades/trade-school-guide/.

Industrial Skilled Trades . "The Skilled Trades Labor Shortage of 2022." *Www.industrialskilledtrades.com*, 22 Feb. 2023, www.industrialskilledtrades.com/skilled-labor-shortage-2022-1.

Ironworker, The Wealthy. "Work - Life Balance and the Skilled Trades - the Wealthy Ironworker Work and Life Balance." *The Wealthy Ironworker*, 16 Dec. 2020, www.thewealthyironworker.com/2020/12/16/work-life-balance-and-the-skilled-trades/. Accessed 5 Sept. 2023.

Irwin, David. "U.S. Skilled Trades Labor Shortage Heightens as In-Demand Jobs Remain Unfilled the Longest." *Www.businesswire.com*, 18 Mar. 2021, www.businesswire.com/news/home/20210318005265/en/U.S.-Skilled-Trades-Labor-Shortage-Heightens-as-In-Demand-Jobs-Remain-Unfilled-the-Longest.

Jeremy Anderberg. "Reviving Blue Collar Work: 5 Benefits of Working in the Skilled Trades." *The Art of Manliness*, 25 Nov. 2014, www.artofmanliness.com/career-wealth/career/reviving-blue-collar-work-5-benefits-of-working-in-the-skilled-trades/.

Kaur, Tanvir. "5 Reasons Why Students Should Explore Careers in Skilled Trades." *Blog.chatterhigh.com*, 26 May 2022, blog.chatterhigh.com/6-reasons-why-students-should-explore-careers-in-skilled-trades.

Kelly, Bridget. "Skilled Trades: A Promising Career Path after High School." *ScholarPath*, 21 Feb. 2023, scholarpath.com/blog/skilled-trades-a-promising-caeer-path/#:~:text=With%20years%20of%20experi-ence%20and. Accessed 5 Sept. 2023.

Lawrence, Amy. "Trade, Tech & Vocational School: What's the Difference?" *Center for Employment Training*, 23 Jan. 2020, cetweb.edu/the-difference-between-trade-schools-vocational-schools-and-tech-schools/.

Mark. "Top 10 Reasons We Love Working in the Trades." *Grade Tech*, 30 July 2020, gradetechservices.com/top-10-reasons-we-love-working-in-the-trades/. Accessed 5 Sept. 2023.

Martins, Ajaero Tony. "25 Best Skilled Trades to Start a Business in 2023." *ProfitableVenture*, 17 May 2022, www.profitableventure.com/best-skilled-trades-start-business/. Accessed 5 Sept. 2023.

McGriff, Margaret . "13 Skilled Trades to Know about | Labor Finders." *Www.laborfinders.com*, 2 Feb. 2022, www.laborfinders.com/blog/list-of-skilled-trades/. Accessed 5 Sept. 2023.

"Most In-Demand Trades for 2021 and beyond — Construction Staffing." *Wideeffect.com*, wideeffect.com/blog/Top+In-Demand+Trades+Jobs+of+2021+and+Beyond/7.

OLSZTYNSKI , JIM . "Most Trade Workers Love Their Jobs." *Explore the Trades*, 25 Oct. 2021, explorethetrades.org/benefits-of-choosing-a-career-in-the-trades/most-trade-workers-love-their-jobs/.

PCI. "What You Need to Apply for Skilled Trades Jobs." *Porter and Chester Institute*, 28 July 2021, porterchester.edu/news-events/skilled-trades-how-build-your-career-portfolio. Accessed 5 Sept. 2023..

"The Demand for Skilled Trades in America." *Ken Rusk*, 14 Mar. 2023, www.kenrusk.com/kens-blog/demand-for-skilled-trades/#:~:text=With%20the%20ongoing%20construction%20boom. Accessed 5 Sept. 2023.

Shockney, Heather. "Balancing Work and Family as a Woman in Skilled Trades." *West Virginia Women Work*, 25 Apr. 2023, westvirginiawomen-work.org/balancing-work-and-family-as-a-woman-in-skilled-trades. Accessed 5 Sept. 2023.

Shook, Justin . "How to Support Mental Health While Working in a Skilled Trade." *SCI*, 2 May 2022, scitexas.edu/blog/how-to-support-mental-health-while-working-in-a-skilled-trade/. Accessed 5 Sept. 2023.

Simmons, Liz . "Top 10 Highest-Paying Trade Jobs." *Www.accreditedschoolson-line.org*, 27 May 2021, www.accreditedschoolsonline.org/vocational-trade-school/highest-paying-trade-jobs/. Accessed 5 Sept. 2023.

"Skilled Trades in America." *Angi Research and Economics*, www.angi.com/re-search/reports/skilled-trades/.

"Skilled Tradespeople Can Power Small Business Growth." *Www.stlouisfed.org*, www.stlouisfed.org/on-the-economy/2018/january/skilled-tradespeople-power-business-growth.

"The 24 Highest-Paying Trade Jobs — No Bachelor's Degree Required." *SkillPointe*, 8 Jan. 2021, skillpointe.com/news-and-advice/24-highest-paying-trade-jobs-no-bachelors-degree-required.

"THE TRADES: FACTS, FIGURES & FUTURE." *Www.tradesnation.com*, www.tradesnation.com/us/en/the-trades-facts-and-figures.html.

"Trade School Scholarships: Free College Grants for Trade School Students." *Collegegrant.net*, 2012, www.collegegrant.net/trade-school-grants/.

"Trade School vs College – How to Decide?" *My College Guide*, mycollegeguide.org/trade-school-vs-college/.

"Trade Schools Guide | Find a College or Vocational School." *Trade-Schools.net*, 2019, www.trade-schools.net/.

Wait, Marianne. "6 Myths about the Skilled Trades." *SkillPointe*, 2 Dec. 2020, skillpointe.com/news-and-advice/6-myths-about-skilled-trades.

Weston, Katelyn Fahrenbruck . "Education after High School: A Guide to College vs. Trade Schools - USCI." *U.S. Career Institute*, www.uscareerinstitute.edu/blog/guide-to-college-vs-trade-school.

"What Are Skilled Trades and Types of Skilled Trade Jobs?" *PTT EDU*, 12 Feb. 2021, ptt.edu/blog/what-jobs-are-considered-skilled-trades/.

"Why You Should Consider a Career in the Skilled Trades." *Lowercolumbia.edu*, lowercolumbia.edu/news/internal/2021/2021-08-06-skilled-trades-careers/. Accessed 21 Mar. 2023.

Wikipedia Contributors. "Collective Bargaining." *Wikipedia*, Wikimedia Foundation, 4 Mar. 2019, en.wikipedia.org/wiki/Collective_bargaining.

"Worker Organizing Resource and Knowledge Center." *Https://Www.workcenter.gov/*, www.workcenter.gov/.

Yee, Sara. " Quotable Quotes: Skilled Trades." Leaderonomics. Last modified September 15, 2021. https://www.leaderonomics.com/articles/personal/quotable-quotes-skilled-trades

Zunch Staffing. "Top 10 Soft Skills Employers Want: Why They Matter and How to Develop Them." *Www.linkedin.com*, www.linkedin.com/pulse/top-10-soft-skills-employers-want-why-matter-how-develop. Accessed 5 Sept. 2023.

Made in the USA
Las Vegas, NV
26 April 2024